To the Littletons
& Hayden
From Grandma
& Grandpa Bill
" Merry Christmas " 1997

CHRISTMAS

Then let every heart keep Christmas within.

Christ's pity for sorrow,

Christ's hatred for sin,

Christ's care for the weakest,

Christ's courage for right.

Everywhere, everywhere, Christmas tonight!

PHILLIPS BROOKS

One of America's most renowned preachers, Phillips Brooks was born in Boston in 1835. Ordained in 1859, he served an Episcopal parish in Philadelphia for ten years. During the winter of 1868, while considering a call to historic Trinity Church in Boston, Brooks wrote the beloved Christmas carol, "O Little Town of Bethlehem." Phillips Brooks died on January 23, 1893.

CHRISTMAS

An Annual Treasury

VOLUME SIXTY–SEVEN

Augsburg
MINNEAPOLIS

Looking Back at Christmas

WHENEVER I THINK BACK TO CHILDHOOD CHRISTMASES IN SOUTHERN Indiana, I remember Christmas Eve. And the highlight of every Christmas Eve was our Sunday school pageant. As we stood in church, reciting pieces from the Christmas story, costumed characters (classmates magically transformed for this one night) enacted that story before our eyes.

First, a young Mary and Joseph made their way down the center aisle to kneel before a straw-filled manger. Soon they were joined by shepherds in bathrobes and wise men wearing paper crowns. After all the characters were in place and our last piece had been spoken, the lights were dimmed and everyone sang "Silent Night" in the glow of a huge Christmas tree. The whole evening was filled with hope and promise.

Even today, Christmas lights and tinsel-covered trees trigger memories of a straw-filled manger, bathrobed shepherds, and young voices reciting, "And it came to pass in those days . . ."

Memories of the past enrich and expand our experience of the present. This year's Annual offers memories of Christmas in America. As you take this nostalgic journey back to earlier days, let the memories draw your family closer to its own past—and to that very first Christmas—and enrich your celebration of this present holy season. Here are some ideas you might try with family and friends.

Hold your own Christmas pageant. Assign pieces from *The Christmas Story* (p. 6) to be recited while characters in simple costumes pantomime the story around your Christmas tree.

Bring together several generations of family and friends to read the Christmas memories in *I Remember Christmas* (p. 10) and enjoy the illustrated nostalgia of *The Christmastime of 50 Years Ago* (p. 47). Then share childhood memories of your own.

Add old and new traditions to special family devotions while trimming the tree, enjoying Christmas breakfast, and welcoming the new year (*Keeping Christmas in the Family*, p. 19).

Gather around the Christmas tree for old-fashioned story time. *The First Christmas Tree* (p. 25) and *How Christmas Came to Blueberry Corners* (p. 40) are perfect read-aloud fare.

The season of Christmas officially lasts until January 6—the festival of Epiphany. So it's not too late to create and give beautiful, hand-crafted gifts that express the joy and meaning of the season (*Simple Gifts*, p. 58).

Wishing you a real old-fashioned Christmas, one that looks all the way back to the manger where Christmas was born.

Bob Klausmeier

EDITOR

Editor: Robert Klausmeier. Art direction, design, production, and layout: Elizabeth Boyce, Craig Claeys, Ellen Maly, David Meyer, Michael Mihelich, and Marti Naughton. Cover art: Ed Parker. Ed Parker is an illustrator living and working in Andover, Massachusetts. He has been represented by Jacqueline Dedell, Inc. since 1988. Frontispiece art: Kenn Backhaus. Photography on pages 15, 55, and 58-63: Leo Kim Photography. With thanks to Beth Harper; Klaus Nurseries, Hastings, Minnesota; Pam McClanahan; Danelle Sweeney; and Rita Thomale.

Library of Congress Catalog Number: 94-74169. International Standard Book Number: 0-8066-8990-0.

Acknowledgments: "The Christmas Story" is taken from the Holy Bible, King James Version. "I Remember Christmas" text copyright © Charles P. Lutz. Used by permission. "Christmas Rainbow" text copyright © Bonnie Compton Hanson. Used by permission. "Christmas Eve in Omaha" text copyright © Jon Hassler. Used by permission. "Keeping Christmas in the Family" text copyright © Debbie Trafton O'Neal. Used by permission. "Journeys" text copyright © Betsy Humphreys. Used by permission. "The Nativity by American Folk Artists" text copyright © Phillip Gugel. Used by permission. "The Christmas I Remember Best" by Rheuama West is reprinted by permission from the *Deseret News*, Salt Lake City, UT. "How Christmas Came to Blueberry Corners" from *Christmas, Volume VII*, text copyright © 1937 Augsburg Publishing House. "The Christmas of 50 Years Ago" from *Christmas, Volume XXII*, text copyright © 1952 Augsburg Publishing House. "The House of Bread" text copyright © Steven Schou. Used by permission. "All Day It's Christmas" from *Christmas in the Big House, Christmas in the Quarters* by Patricia C. McKissack and Fredrick L. McKissack, text copyright © 1994 Patricia C. McKissack and Fredrick L. McKissack. Used by permission of Scholastic, Inc. Introductions to stories by Lois Lenski and Eugene Field partially excerpted from *Journey Into Childhood: The Autobiography of Lois Lenski*, Lippincott, 1972; and *Field Days: The Life, Times and Reputation* of Eugene Field by Robert Conrow, Scribner, 1974.

Contents

page 40

page 38

page 19

The Christmas Story

ACCORDING TO ST. LUKE AND ST. MATTHEW

AND IN THE SIXTH MONTH THE ANGEL GABRIEL was sent from God unto a city of Galilee, named Nazareth, to a virgin espoused to a man whose name was Joseph, of the house of David; and the virgin's name was Mary.

And the angel came in unto her, and said, "Hail, thou that art highly favored, the Lord is with thee: blessed art thou among women."

And when she saw him, she was troubled at his saying, and cast in her mind what manner of salutation this should be.

And the angel said unto her, "Fear not, Mary: for thou hast found favor with God. And, behold, thou shalt conceive in thy womb, and bring forth a son, and shalt call his name Jesus. He shall be great, and shall be called the Son of the Highest: and the Lord God shall give unto him the throne of his father David:

and he shall reign over the house of Jacob for ever; and of his kingdom there shall be no end.

Then said Mary unto the angel, "How shall this be, seeing I know not a man?"

And the angel answered and said unto her, "The Holy Ghost shall come upon thee, and the power of the Highest shall overshadow thee: therefore also that holy thing which shall be born of thee shall be called the Son of God.

"And, behold, thy cousin Elisabeth, she hath also conceived a son in her old age: and this is the sixth month with her, who was called barren. For with God nothing shall be impossible."

And Mary said, "Behold the handmaid of the Lord; be it unto me according to thy word. And the angel departed from her.

And it came to pass in those days, that there went out a decree from Caesar Augustus, that all the world should be taxed. And this taxing was first made when Cyrenius was governor of Syria. And all went to be taxed, every one into his own city.

And Joseph also went up from Galilee, out of the city of Nazareth, into Judaea, unto the city of David, which is called Bethlehem; because he was of the house and lineage of David: to be taxed with Mary his espoused wife, being great with child.

And so it was, that, while they were there, the days were accomplished that she should be delivered.

And she brought forth her firstborn son, and wrapped him in swaddling clothes, and laid him in a manger; because there was no room for them in the inn.

And there were in the same country shepherds abiding in the field, keeping watch over their flock by night. And, lo, the angel of the Lord came upon them, and the glory of the Lord shone round about them: and they were sore afraid.

And the angel said unto them, "Fear not: for, behold, I bring you good tidings of great joy, which shall be to all people. For unto you is born this day in the city of David a Savior, which is Christ the Lord. And this shall be a sign unto you; ye shall find the babe wrapped in swaddling clothes, lying in a manger."

And suddenly there was with the angel a multitude of the heavenly host praising God, and saying, "Glory to God in the highest, and on earth peace, good will toward men."

And it came to pass, as the angels were gone away from them into heaven, the shepherds said one to another, "Let us now go even unto Bethlehem, and see this thing which is come to pass, which the Lord hath made known unto us."

And they came with haste, and found Mary, and Joseph, and the babe lying in a manger. And when they had seen it, they made known abroad the saying which was told them concerning this child. And all they that heard it wondered at those things which were told them by the shepherds. But Mary kept all these things, and pondered them in her heart. And the shepherds returned, glorifying and praising God for all the things that they had heard and seen, as it was told unto them.

Now when Jesus was born in Bethlehem of Judaea in the days of Herod the king, behold, there came wise men from the east to Jerusalem, saying, "Where is he that is born King of the Jews? For we have seen his star in the east, and are come to worship him."

When Herod the king had heard these things, he was troubled, and all Jerusalem with him. And when he had gathered all the chief priests and scribes of the people together, he demanded of them where Christ should be born.

And they said unto him, "In Bethlehem of Judaea: for thus it is written by the prophet, 'And thou Bethlehem, in the land of Juda, art not the least among the princes of Juda: for out of thee shall come a Governor, that shall rule my people Israel.'"

Then Herod, when he had privily called the wise men, enquired of them diligently what time the star appeared. And he sent them to Bethlehem, and said, "Go and search diligently for the young child; and when ye have found him, bring me word again, that I may come and worship him also."

When they had heard the king, they departed; and, lo, the star, which they saw in the east, went before them, till it came and stood over where the young child was. When they saw the star, they rejoiced with exceeding great joy.

And when they were come into the house, they saw the young child with Mary his mother, and fell down, and worshiped him: and when they had opened their treasures, they presented unto him gifts; gold, and frankincense, and myrrh.

And being warned of God in a dream that they should not return to Herod, they departed into their own country another way.

Shola Friedensohn is a graphic designer and freelance illustrator living in Cambridge, Massachusetts. She writes: "I drew the angels on an enormous scale because I imagine that being visited by an angel of God must be a tremendous and awe-inspiring event. The first angel is a very private angel, appearing at twilight, only to Mary. The second angel is a messenger of light for all the world, perhaps like the Aurora Borealis. In bringing the observer up close to both illustrations I wanted to emphasize the contrast between the angels and the very human intimacy of the holy family and the three kings."

❧ I Remember Christmas ❧

Reflections on Childhood Holidays of the Past

CHARLES P. LUTZ

CHRISTMAS IN THE EARLY YEARS of the Twentieth Century was a far cry from today's celebrations. It was a time when few families had automobiles, when many lived on farms and getting to a church in town was a major undertaking, when lighted candles on trees were common despite the danger of fires. And the biting cold weather, coupled with inadequate heating systems, left impressions that are powerful to this day. Fifteen people who were born near the turn of the century shared memories of those early times as they reminisced about childhood Christmases and Christmas pageants.

British author James M. Barrie once wrote: "God gave us memories so we could have roses in the Decembers of our lives." Here, in the reflections of those fifteen men and women, are some rich roses from Decembers of long ago.

Mildred Holcomb, born in 1903, recalled Christmas pageant rehearsals at a country church in Kossuth County, Iowa. She shared these memories in 1982 with members of First Lutheran Church, St. Peter, Minnesota, where she was a member until her death in 1996.

We knew what was waiting for us inside the church during the rehearsals: icy cold! When there was a meeting for adults, someone would get a good fire burning. For children it was not considered so important. So we kept our coats and boots on, and our fascinators stayed wrapped tightly around our throats.

The rehearsal started just as soon as the minister came from the parsonage next door. He would stay at the rear of the church and prance back and forth, shouting "Louder, you!" at the shivering, cringing lostling standing alone up in front of the altar.

Of course there was always the "Rhodes scholar" every year. He could speak his piece loudly and clearly and, in the view of the congregation, was naturally destined to become a pastor. Sometimes a girl would outdo the others, but this was not considered important. Her calling was to be a good wife and mother, nothing else.

We would stop for a half hour to eat our lunch of frozen sandwiches and then go back to practice again. The rehearsal was over when our parents came and took us home—to a cold house. But it wasn't long before the house got warm, and so did we.

Jewell Haaland of rural Cottonwood, Minnesota, was born on March 28, 1910. He spent his life farming in Minnesota's Yellow Medicine County near the South Dakota border.

The Christmas Eve program at church was the biggest event of the year. All of us children had to say a piece from the Christmas story—in Norwegian. After the program, the congregation gave each child an apple and a bag of peanuts.

Our farm was six miles away from the church. The entire family, usually a dozen or more, would travel to the program by horse-drawn bobsled. The trip took more than an hour, and it was cold. To keep warm, we'd put our feet on large stones that had been warmed all day in our kitchen oven and placed beneath blankets in the sled.

The childhood Christmas gift I remember most fondly came from one of my married brothers. It was a newborn puppy. I remember thinking how much nicer that was than the usual gifts of clothing.

Eugene J. McCarthy, born March 29, 1916, spent his childhood in Watkins, Minnesota. He served in the U. S. House of Representatives from 1949-59, and in the U. S. Senate from 1959-71; and he was a Presidential candidate in 1968. McCarthy now lives in the Washington, D. C. area.

Watkins, Minnesota and St. Anthony's Catholic Church had a definite German character, even into the late 1920s. Sermons were given in both German and English, as were confessions, although absolution was always in Latin.

I recall the Feast of St. Nicholas (December 6) being in some ways more memorable than Christmas. This was because Black Peter appeared—well, was heard from, anyway—to warn children to be good, at least until Christmas. The rest of our Christmas observances were largely traditional, with midnight Mass as the central act.

Presents under Christmas trees were not wrapped in fancy paper. For children there were toys, one or two of which would not survive much beyond the Christmas season. A drum for a boy, perhaps, which would not last long and probably be the last drum he'd ever receive. There would also be a gift of winter clothes, woolen and warm.

Dorothy Haas spent 42 years in religious education with parishes and in national executive positions with Lutheran women's organizations and the American Bible Society. She was born July 12, 1907, in Ann Arbor, Michigan and lives today in Minneapolis.

I am an only child, also the only grandchild on my mother's side, so I was well-favored at Christmastime. But I always wanted so badly to share with other children, especially at Christmas.

One day, when I was five, I accompanied my mother to a Lutheran orphans' home in Toledo, Ohio. I asked if we could take one of the young children to our home in Ann Arbor for Christmas. We were told that a four-year-old boy, Dale, had no family and he could spend a few days with us. I was in heaven.

Dale got to be part of our family tree trimming and gift opening Christmas morning, as well as going to worship with us. We took him back to Toledo a few days later. Coming home without him was the saddest day of my young life.

Then, some years later, another family in our parish adopted Dale. I was ecstatic. I became "Aunt Dorothy" to him and later to his children. I just knew it all happened because God answered my Christmastime prayers of several years before.

Esther Wesner was born in Norway on May 20, 1903 and moved to St. Paul when she was four years old. After a career in office work for the state government, she continues to live in St. Paul.

Since our 1907 arrival in St. Paul, I've been a member of Christ Lutheran Church near the State Capitol. Our Sunday school Christmas program was usually on the Sunday evening after Christmas Day. When I was about six, I was chosen to speak the Julevangelium (Christmas story) in Norwegian. It was a special honor. I memorized it and practiced over and over. Later I was told that many in the congregation cried because my Norwegian was so good.

At the Christmas Eve dinner in our home, we always left some food for the nisser—the elves who would be coming to visit during the night. I suppose our parents cleared the table after we children were asleep. But in the morning when the food was gone, we children knew that the nisser had visited.

Noah Brokenleg was born July 4, 1913 in Rosebud, South Dakota. An archdeacon of the Episcopal Church, he served communities on the Pine Ridge and Rosebud Reservations. Brokenleg now lives in Mission, South Dakota.

When I was six or seven, I remember going to a small white church near Parmelee for Christmas services. A large cedar tree was up front by the altar. One side of the tree was decorated and draped with blue woolen cloth unwrapped from a bolt; the remainder of the bolt was at the base of the tree. The other side of the tree was draped in the same way with another cloth—flowered and shiny. Candles were burning on the tree, and two men stood nearby with pails of water in case fire started.

A lay reader led the service, talking about the birthday of a Child named Jesus. Prayers and singing were in our Lakota language. On the wall, made from cedar branches, were a circle, a triangle, and a cross—adults spoke about the meaning of those symbols.

After the service, toys and bags of candy, fruit, and nuts were given to all; but we were cautioned not to eat in church. The bolts of cloth were cut into lengths and given to the women for dress material.

Families were camping in wall tents around the church, which was on the Rosebud Reservation. Nearly all came by team and wagon, bringing along hay, grain, and blankets for the horses, and firewood for the tent stoves. That night, somehow we didn't seem to notice the cold weather.

Harold Stassen was born April 13, 1907 in St. Paul Minnesota. Elected governor of Minnesota at the age of 31, he was a chief drafter of the United Nations Charter (1945) and is its sole surviving signer. Several times a Presidential candidate, Stassen lives today in Sunfish Lake, Minnesota.

In our Baptist church we had an annual Christmas program with recitations by all the children. Both my wife, Esther, and I participated from the age of five onward. Today we are members of Riverview Baptist Church in West St. Paul, Minnesota.

Oletta Wald, born August 22, 1908, spent most of her childhood in Slater, Iowa. She taught in Minnesota public schools and at Lutheran Bible Institute in Minneapolis and developed religious education curriculum. She now lives in Minneapolis.

My early Christmas memories come from central Iowa. Our little town had three Norwegian Lutheran churches. My church was the smallest and least liturgical and had a visiting pastor who conducted worship just once a month. Corn farmers led services the other Sundays. All were in Norwegian, which I didn't understand, so I never went to worship as a child. But I did get to Sunday school, which was in English.

Neither our church nor our town made much of Christmas. The Fourth of July was the big celebration. I recall going to Christmas programs with cousins at Slater's Methodist Church, and that's where I received my bag of candy.

My mother was a widow with eight children; Father had died before I was born. We were poor, and the only way we were able to have a Christmas tree was by getting the public school's tree when Christmas vacation came. Even though our material gifts were few, I received from my mother and my Sunday school teacher a deep sense of peace and security in the Christmas gospel message that God loves his people.

Alta Lewis was born on Christmas Day in 1899 in Indianapolis. She worked at Minnesota Mutual Life for 41 years and now lives in St. Paul.

I've always felt it was a privilege to be born on our Lord's birthday. I certainly never felt deprived as a child because Christmas and my birthday fell on the same day. My family always tried to treat all the children fairly.

After we moved to St. Paul in 1908, I remember walking to school past the excavation for the new Catholic cathedral. My siblings and I were sometimes late for school because we were so fascinated by the digging. We were members at Emmanuel Baptist and later at the Christian and Missionary Alliance Church, where I'm still a member.

As children we had to practice our pieces for the church Christmas program over and over so we could say them with no mistakes. But then, when the time came, we always seemed to get tongue-tied anyway.

Sam King was born September 4, 1915 and spent his childhood in Pittsburgh, where he attended an African-American Methodist church. After military service in World War II, he worked for thirty-seven years with the Veterans Administration in New York, Chicago, and St. Paul. King now lives in St. Paul.

Sunday school Christmas plays were a big thing in my childhood church. All the children had short pieces to say. But the folks in charge knew better than to ask me to sing. Even though my mother played the organ at our church, singing was not one of my gifts. And everyone knew it. We always got a bag of hard candy from the church after the plays.

I remember Christmas in our home as a time of abundance, a time filled with things we didn't have normally, like fresh fruit and nuts and turkey and goose. Gifts were mainly books. We had an uncle who was a fanatic about books. And I've always been grateful for that.

Katherine Morken was born on a farm in O'Brien County in northwest Iowa in 1904. While raising three children, she operated a restaurant in Frazee, Minnesota. She now lives in Minneapolis.

We farmed several miles from the town of Sutherland, Iowa. Since we had to travel by horse and buggy—or else walk—we seldom got to town for anything, including church. The minister came around to the rural homes for pastoral services, even for baptisms.

So my early memories of Christmas are from our home. About a week before Christmas, each child would hang up a stocking in which candy would appear every morning. Santa always came to visit on Christmas Eve. (We later discovered it was our father.) I also remember groups going around caroling and being invited in for sweets.

My parents, who came from Germany, insisted we speak only German at home. But school was in English, so my older brothers and sisters secretly took me into the woods on our farm to teach me English before I started school. When I was ten, we moved to Becker County, Minnesota, to farm in what was a Norwegian community. Then we got to church more regularly, but only on alternate Sundays when they had English services. I remember the Norwegians staring at us as though we were foreigners.

Olga Lutz was born on June 2, 1909 near Andrew in Jackson County, eastern Iowa. An office secretary, pastor's wife, writer, and mother of six, she now lives in Minneapolis.

Christmas Eve at Salem Lutheran Church in Andrew was the biggest thing every year in the lives of us all, children and adults. It was the fullest church service of the entire year. We always had a native tree with candles. It stood in a side balcony, and a man sat nearby with a pail of water. Each child had a piece to memorize, and each received a book and a bag of candy, fruit, and nuts from the congregation.

Our family gift exchange was on December 23 so we children could have our new clothes to wear to church on Christmas Eve. There was always a Christmas Day service, too. All services were in German, but Sunday school and the Christmas Eve program were in English.

We traveled to church by horse-drawn cutter, an open sleigh with two seats. (Our first family automobile came in 1915 when I was six.) It was ten miles to church, and the trip took us about an hour each way. I recall once being upset in a snow drift, but no one was hurt, and we made it to church safe and sound.

Douglas Racine was born September 25, 1900 in Little Canada, Minnesota. After spending his entire work life with Northern States Power in the Twin Cities, Racine now lives in St. Paul.

The altar area of my childhood church, St. John's Roman Catholic in Little Canada, was brightly decorated with holly and pine branches, plus lighted candles. The children in the parish would be asked to sing and act out parts from the Christmas gospel. I could sing real loud, but I couldn't carry a tune. So they always asked me to please just move my lips—which I did.

I remember when I was about nine, I overheard my older sisters wrapping gifts and talking. I was in my upstairs bedroom and I could hear their voices through the register that was open for heat to rise. They were talking about surprising us younger ones with Santa Claus. That's when I found out Santa did not exist. I resolved not to spoil it for my younger brother, who was then four. I succeeded in keeping the secret from him for several more years.

Theodore Fricke of Edina, Minnesota was born in Detroit on December 21, 1904. He was a Lutheran parish pastor in Michigan, Ohio, and the District of Columbia, before serving as world mission executive with national Lutheran church bodies.

When I was nine, I was given "Away in a Manger" to sing in our church Christmas program. I knew the song perfectly, but for some reason got started an octave too high. I remember looking out at my mother; her face confirmed that I had a problem. But instead of starting over, I squeaked my way through it. Afterwards I vowed never again to solo in public, and I haven't.

The childhood Christmas I remember best was 1908. On December 8, my dad, who was helping build an industrial smokestack in Mayville, Wisconsin, was killed when a scaffold fell. I was not yet four. I can still see the casket in our Detroit parlor, right next to the Christmas tree. I've always been thankful to my mother for seeing to it that, even as we were saying farewell to our father, we children could still celebrate Christmas.

Mom was a strong woman with a vibrant faith. She made Christmas that year a time of triumph for herself and for all of us children.

Conrad Bergendoff was born December 3, 1895. He looks forward to his 102nd Christmas this year in Rock Island, Illinois. His career as a theologian and academic leader included several decades as the president of Augustana College and Seminary in Rock Island.

Christmas in the congregation of my childhood centered around the tall tree in the sanctuary. Trimming it was the beginning. Real candles were essential, even with the risk of fire (which called for safeguards).

Julotta (the Swedish Christmas morning service) at 5 a.m. was traditional, when choirs and music dominated. The church glowed with candles and greenery. Sunday school Christmas was a program where children took part.

From Advent to Epiphany, the church made Christmas a memory for life. Echoes of the music especially lingered long. My memories go back to Middletown, Connecticut, where Father was pastor from 1900-1912. Since then I have celebrated Christmas in Chicago, Rock Island, Philadelphia, and Sweden. In all these places, for over a century, the celebration has had many similar elements. And always, everywhere, the message: "Christ is born in Bethlehem!"

Charles P. Lutz is editor emeritus of *Metro Lutheran*, a monthly newspaper published in Minneapolis. He retired in 1996 after 40 years in professional church work as a journalist and social ministry specialist. He lives in Minneapolis.

Christmas Rainbow

BONNIE COMPTON HANSON

As golden as tinsel and tassels,
As golden as balls that delight,
As golden as starlight and angels,
The Babe of that first Christmas night.

As green as the gay-berried holly,
As green as the bright mistletoe,
As green as the spruce and the cypress,
The life that Christ lived here below.

As red as a cold winter sunset,
As red as poinsettia tree,
As red as a fire's dying embers,
The blood that my Lord shed for me.

As white as the snow silent falling,
As white as a frost-fettered leaf,
As white as the cold breath of winter,
The tomb where they laid Him in grief.

Oh, spread out the green and the golden,
The red and the white show in love,
For the Babe that they honor at Christmas
Is our Lord who is reigning above!

Bonnie Compton Hanson, of Santa Ana, California, writes: "Cleaning out my garage one August afternoon, I discovered a misplaced bag of Christmas decorations. When I emptied it, out spilled a rainbow of well-worn but treasured glass balls—gold, red, green, and white. As their out-of-season beauty sparkled in the summer sun, this poem spilled out, as well. What joy that the wonder of Christ's coming need not be confined to just one day, month, or season, but can be shared all year long!"

A YOUNG MAN'S CHRISTMAS WITH HIS GRANDPARENTS IS COLORED BY MYTHS AND MEMORIES OF HIS FATHER.

Christmas Eve in Omaha

JON HASSLER

Novelist Jon Hassler is professor of English at St. John's University in Collegeville, Minnesota. His story, "Christmas Eve in Omaha" first appeared in Image: A Journal of the Arts and Religion. *Hassler writes about his contribution to* Christmas: *"I believe a story is not complete until the reader has read it. We react to a story based on the experience we bring to it, and only then does the story become complete. In casting about for a story to provoke reader reaction, I have settled more than once on Christmas as a theme. For what is more provocative than the bittersweet memories of Christmas? This particular story is based on an experience my wife told me concerning her sister who served in the USO during World War II. My wife's strongest memory of that time is of a record sent home from the USO on which her sister was singing 'I'll Be Home for Christmas.' I asked my wife if her sister did come home for Christmas. She said she didn't remember. And with that little germ of an idea, I wrote 'Christmas Eve in Omaha' with Leland Edwards at its center. The story is now part of a novel about Leland Edwards,* The Dean's List, *which was published in May."*

W E DROVE TO NEBRASKA EVERY CHRISTMAS FOR MANY YEARS, Mother and I, continuing a practice begun when I was a boy and my father was still alive. We stopped first in Omaha to spend a rather stiff, unfestive Christmas Eve with my father's family, the Edwardses, and then early the next morning went on to a ranch further west where we had a jolly time with my mother's people, the O'Kellys.

Not that the Edwardses were unkind or inhospitable. It's only that mother's relatives were much more spontaneous and high-spirited by nature. At Christmas dinner the O'Kellys specialized in stories so uproarious they must have been invented, although they often began or ended with the phrase, "Swear to God." And after dinner, even more aunts and uncles and cousins came pouring through the house to greet us. Any given Christmas, we probably saw thirty-five O'Kellys.

16

Christmas Eve in Omaha was observed with fewer people, and mostly without laughter. An Edwards conversation followed a predictable line, beginning with the unreliability of the weather and leading on through the deteriorating condition of their aging automobiles and their ailing friends and neighbors. As a young man I used to consider this talk painfully dull, but over the years I learned to take a certain pleasure in the constancy of it, the way you will sometimes come to appreciate a cheerless old hymn in church simply because it is so familiar. I suppose, as we age, any sign of permanence consoles us, no matter if it bores us besides.

I find it curious that despite the high colors of the O'Kelly Christmases, the Edwardses, as a family, are more clearly etched in my boyhood memories. Grandfather Edwards, a small man with a mustache and a hearing aid, was made to seem even smaller by the engulfing overstuffed chair he always sat in. "Come, Leland, we'll read," he used to declare, and I would climb up on his lap and be read to from a book of moralizing tales about a boy named Henry.

I remember Grandmother Edwards setting seven places at the table, for we were always joined by Aunt Cora, Uncle Herbert, and their son Wesley, who lived nearby. Uncle Herbert was a butcher. Cousin Wesley was mischievous, and I never liked him very much. Grandmother would sit at the foot of the table, silently nibbling and smiling at me whenever our eyes met.

This smile, never quite joyous, turned very sad the year I was eight and my father was stationed in California and waiting to be shipped out to the war in the South Pacific. I recall the phonograph record he sent home to his parents that winter. Although he'd printed a message on the back of the envelope—"Don't open without Lolly and Leland present"—Cousin Wesley was discovered opening it before we got there. It was unlike any record we had ever seen—small, thin, bendable, and nearly transparent, with grooves only on one side. It had a red, white, and blue label on which was printed "U.S.O. San Francisco."

Grandfather set it on the spindle, lowered the needle, and we were all astonished to hear my father's voice. He was singing, a cappella, "I'll Be Home for Christmas." Mother laughed and wept. Grandmother only wept. I felt supremely triumphant, for not only did Wesley's father have no singing voice, he'd also been rejected as physically unfit for the armed forces. We played the record again and again, far into the night.

The following Christmas season, a glimmer of joy appeared in Grandmother Edwards' smile, for my father was safely home. But five years later—I was fourteen—the smile turned severely sad again, and stayed that way for the rest of her life. That was the year my father was killed by lightning while fishing from a canoe.

Of course Mother and I, too, were devastated. Over time, Mother gradually recovered, calling on inner resources I didn't seem to have. She began to laugh once more, and I resented her laughter. As an introspective and only child, I'd never found it easy to make friends, and so my father had been my closest chum. Fortunately, he'd left me a legacy of absorbing hobbies—fishing, stamp-collecting, playing the piano—and these I pursued with a kind of mad intensity; yet I could never quite throw off the gloom I felt whenever it occurred to me that I must go on living in a world bereft of my dear father.

Too bad that a tragedy of that magnitude was required to bring me into a closer union with my father's family, but that's what happened. I acquired an affinity for—indeed, I found myself imitating—the Edwards' reticence, their measured, mournful ways. True, I still enjoyed Christmas Day on the O'Kelly ranch, but I found myself looking forward more eagerly to Christmas Eve in Omaha, where my father's memory was held in sacred trust.

When, with time, my memories of my father began to fade, my melancholy did not. It was compounded, in fact, by guilt. I wanted to be able to dwell on his life the way they did in Omaha. So intense was their devotion that I began to feel extremely unworthy. In retrospect, of course, I see that my common sense was telling me to quit probing my wound and get on with my life, but to do so at the time would have seemed a kind of betrayal. It took the upheaval of a moving day to shake me out of this state of unhealthy nostalgia.

I think it was my twenty-sixth Christmas when my grandparents decided to leave their house in Omaha and take a suburban apartment. In planning to be packed and moved by Christmas Eve, they'd overestimated not only their endurance but also the hours of help Cousin Wesley was to give them. And when Mother and I arrived around noon, we found Grandfather exhausted and deeply asleep in his overstuffed chair, Grandmother full of tearful apologies, and the house in disarray—curtains down, cupboards half empty, dozens of half-packed boxes scattered through the rooms. Soon Wesley arrived with his parents and his pickup, and we all pitched in, working far into the evening and getting about half their belongings moved into the apartment before all of us wore out.

Christmas Eve dinner was takeout Chinese, eaten around midnight. We were sipping coffee and munching Aunt Cora's holiday cookies, when I brought out the celluloid record of my father's voice. Earlier, while working with Grandmother in the attic, I'd come across it in a hatbox of mementos. I put it on the turntable. The sound was amazingly clear, his voice so wonderfully fresh and melodious that he seemed to be present in the room. "I'll be home for Christmas," he sang, and we sat there enchanted. I played it a second time, and we exchanged a few reverent remarks. I played it a third time, and each of us gazed off in a private direction, calling up private memories. Even Cousin Wesley seemed moved.

I switched it off then, and a curious conversation ensued. It began with Grandfather, who declared "Typical of that boy not to say it right out that he was coming home."

"Yes, that was his sweet way," said Aunt Cora, concerning her brother. "Tell us in a song like that. And the next thing, there he was."

"Typical," Grandfather repeated, as though the memory irked him. "Surprise you like that. Never say it straight out."

Uncle Herbert agreed. "Just gave us that one clue."

"But he didn't . . ." began Grandmother, her memory evidently clearer than theirs, but she was not given a chance to finish. Aunt Cora was remembering the gifts he'd brought from Hawaii:

"To this day I keep the Pearl Harbor pillow on the daybed. And Wesley, don't you still carry that jackknife?"

Cousin Wesley said he did.

Aunt Cora turned to Mother. "Lolly, you must've been the most surprised of all when he showed up. You and Leland."

Mother and I exchanged a look, and before she could point out that they had their Christmas memories mixed up, Aunt Cora was going on:

"Or did you and Leland know ahead of time and not tell us?"

"Seems like yesterday," said Uncle Herbert.

"I thought he'd be in uniform, but he wasn't," said Wesley.

Grandmother timidly made another attempt. "I don't think he came home that Christmas . . ."

And Mother came to her aid. "It was the following year he brought the things from Hawaii."

Grandfather declared both of them mistaken. First the record appeared, then my father himself, the same day. Wesley and his parents all nodded their support.

"Oh, so that's how it was," said Grandmother, and I watched a smile spread across her face as she allowed herself to believe this erroneous version. It made such a pleasing story after all.

I spoke up then, pointing out that the song wasn't about actually coming home for Christmas—only dreaming about it.

Mother, too, persisted, repeating the facts—the record one Christmas, his homecoming the next.

None of this made an impression on them. With Grandmother forsaking the truth and going over to the other side, we were outnumbered five to two. There was a moment or two of strain—a kind of silent standoff—before Mother laughed and said, "What difference does it make? At least we have his voice. Would you play it again, Leland?"

And so we listened once more, all of us sitting there in a kind of stupor of satisfaction: Grandfather, Aunt Cora, Uncle Herbert and Wesley happily picturing the day they'd invented; Grandmother putting their invention together, piece by piece, in her imagination; Mother not caring what they thought, only relishing in the sound of the voice preserved so fortuitously by the U.S.O., San Francisco.

And I, of course, was relieved beyond measure as I watched a pleasing myth replace the less dramatic facts, and I saw how trivial were the memories I'd been trying so hard to preserve.

Memories, fading and flawed, were all they had in Omaha, while I had my father's fishing tackle, his stamp collection, his sheet music. Like him, I was a school teacher. I lived in his house. I had his knack for catching walleyes. I didn't have his singing voice, but I had his talent at the piano. I had his way of walking, said Mother, with my left foot slightly splayed. I knew from photographs that I had his forehead and eyes. And I had this family of his, who, I sensed, would go on worshiping his memory over the years, preserving it, in their way, from oblivion, while I went ahead and lived the life he lost. ❦

Illustrator Bob Crofut entitles his work "An American Remembrance" and in it seeks to evoke a sense of our past American experience. He writes: "In my work I try to evoke a feeling for people and places that are real, but softened by memory. It is a look I've found lends itself to the expression of our hopes, struggles, and dreams." Crofut lives and works in a converted carriage house in Ridgefield, Connecticut.

TRADITIONS, ACTIVITIES, PRAYERS, AND CAROLS
THREE DEVOTIONS FOR THE CHRISTMAS SEASON

Keeping Christmas in the Family

DEBBIE TRAFTON O'NEAL

THERE'S NOTHING QUITE LIKE AN AMERICAN CHRISTMAS. Of course, our celebration is usually a combination of traditions and festivities that come from other countries. But that is one of the great things about it—the wonderful way all kinds of foods, customs, and traditions are blended to create a uniquely American flavor.

Have you ever thought about where some of your family's favorite holiday customs come from? If not, perhaps this will be a good year to do so, as you build your own unique ways of celebrating the holidays. Record favorite recipes, customs, songs, and other seasonal observances in a year-by-year Christmas journal. Be sure to add the origins of the customs. Do some research, if necessary. Through the years, as you add new festivities and foods to your celebrations, include them in your family Christmas book.

GATHER 'ROUND THE TREE: A DEVOTION FOR CHRISTMAS EVE

As Christmas Day approaches, we prepare for the Christ child's birth—within our homes and within our hearts. My family finds the perfect tree to trim, assembles our nativity set, puts favorite holiday books in a basket by the fireplace, and selects Christmas music to play and sing together.

Tree trimming is a wonderful tradition, a time for joy and reminiscing as family members ooh and ahh over ornaments they have collected through the years. Our family has one very special ornament, an empty bird's nest we discovered after cutting a fresh tree one Christmas years ago. It was nestled near the top branches, so close to the trunk that we didn't discover it until we had returned home. It was the first decoration we added to that tree. And every Christmas since, after tenderly removing it from its wrapping, we give it the place of honor on our tree. With a little research, I discovered that a bird's nest found in a Christmas tree means a new year of good fortune!

If possible, purchase or make a small bird's nest ornament (or a tiny basket) to place on your tree. Then gather around the Christmas tree and give each family member a slip of paper on which to write the name of a person they want to pray for at this time of year. Turn off all the lights in the room except those on the tree.

Leader 1: Thank you, dear God, for this time when we can join our hearts and hands as a family. As we look around this circle, help us remember all the people in our family—those here with us now, those who are in other homes and cities, and those who have gone before us. Thank you especially for . . . (*each person names a family member—don't forget uncles, aunts, grandparents, and great-grandparents*).

Leader 2: Thank you, dear God, for the traditions and customs our family has shared through the years. (*Name some Christmas traditions you have carried over from your childhood, and invite children to mention customs they love.*)

As we add our special prayer slips to the Christmas tree, bless those whom we have named during this holy season. Amen. (*Pass the nest around so each person can place a prayer slip inside it. Then place the nest on one of the top branches of the tree.*)

Serve cups of spiced cider or hot cocoa stirred with a peppermint stick. As you sip, take turns sharing memories of past Christmas Eves. Adults can recall meaningful or amusing incidents from their childhood. Children will enjoy telling about special memories from their "childhood," too. Top off the evening by reading the Christmas story in St. Luke's Gospel and join in singing "I Am So Glad Each Christmas Eve." (p. 23)

CELEBRATE THE DAY: A DEVOTION FOR CHRISTMAS MORNING

The excitement of Christmas morning! The smell of cardamom, cinnamon, and nutmeg mingling with the scent of pine needles; the sounds of laughter as gifts are unwrapped; the cozy feeling of sitting together over coffee, hot cocoa, and spiced, braided Christmas bread.

Many of my family traditions are Scandinavian. So, on Christmas morning, we share warm Scandinavian coffee bread, flavored with cardamom, braided into a wreath, and topped with white icing and red and green candied cherries. We also share a dish of rice pudding with a sauce made of dried fruits. Tradition has it that the person who finds an almond in his or her sauce will have good luck in the coming year. When my children were small, we added a new twist to the tradition: the person who finds the almond must create a unique ornament to give the person who finds the almond the following year. This has become one of our favorite holiday traditions.

Every country has a special bread or holiday cake recipe. Find one that comes from your family's heritage and prepare it for Christmas morning. If possible, shape the bread into a festive wreath, tree, or candy cane. Make a pot of something warm to drink with the bread. Then gather at the table to begin the special day of Christ's birth.

Leader 1: We welcome the morning, Lord. Especially this morning when we celebrate the birth of Jesus. Thank you for bringing us safely through the night, for giving us the stars that light our night, the sun that cheers our day, and the most precious gift of all, your Son. We also thank you, God, for . . . (*allow time for family members to share their thanks*).

Leader 2: (*Holding up the bread*) Dear God, you always give us our daily bread. Thank you for this special bread that reminds us of our family traditions and the family members who have gone before us. Even though they are not with us today, we remember them and we thank you for them. Amen.

As you enjoy your Christmas breakfast, play favorite Christmas tapes or CDs and share family stories from the past—childhood memories, the kind of Christmas your grandparents celebrated, how your ancestors came to America. Then gather around a nativity set to sing the lovely carol, "Away in a Manger." (p. 23)

A NEW BEGINNING: A DEVOTION FOR NEW YEAR'S DAY

Although New Year's Day is not a religious holiday, it is an ideal time for Christians to celebrate with prayers and songs as they reflect on the past and make plans for the coming year.

We have the tradition of gathering with other families at one of our homes for a New Year's open-house buffet. There are lots of goodies to munch on and games to play, as well as football games for those who want to watch them. One family adds another activity to their New Year's Day: sorting through photographs taken during the past year and adding them to photo albums. They also look at albums from previous years to see how people have changed and grown. This is a wonderful way to recall God's blessings of the past.

Here's one New Year's Day tradition you might add to your celebrations with family or friends. Set a basket full of index cards, blank envelopes, pens, and pencils in the center of the table. Everyone can write his or her name on one of the envelopes and then place these, name-up, near the basket. Next, let everyone take a card for each person in the family—themselves included. Think of one goal or achievement each family member will accomplish during the coming year, and write this on a card. Then write a brief prayer for that person. Place completed cards into the labeled envelopes. When everyone is finished, seal the envelopes, date them, and put them away to be opened next New Year's Day. What fun it will be to see how many goals were reached and how many prayers were answered!

Leader 1: (*Place basket with the sealed envelopes in the center of the table.*) Dear Lord, thank you for this new day and this new year. In this basket are loving thoughts, hopes, and prayers for all gathered here today.

Leader 2: Take these thoughts, hopes, and prayers, and bless them, Lord. Whatever the coming year brings, help us remember that we have your love to guide us and the love of our family and friends to give us strength and support. May all we do and say in this new year be a reflection of our love for one another and our faith in you. Amen.

As the time of holiday celebration comes to a close, join in singing the traditional American spiritual, "Go Tell It on the Mountain" (p. 24). As you sing the words, think about ways your words and actions will tell others about the Son of God, whose birth you have celebrated.

I AM SO GLAD EACH CHRISTMAS EVE

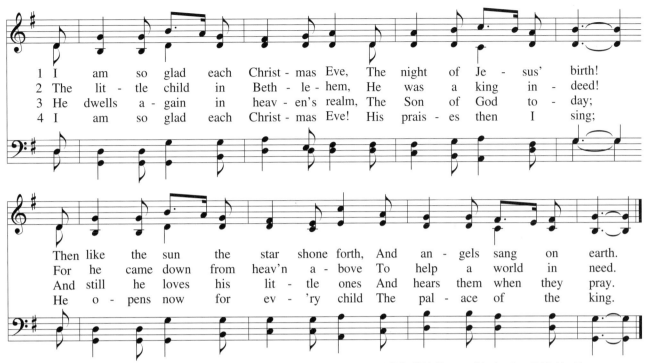

1 I am so glad each Christ - mas Eve, The night of Je - sus' birth!
2 The lit - tle child in Beth - le - hem, He was a king in - deed!
3 He dwells a - gain in heav - en's realm, The Son of God to - day;
4 I am so glad each Christ - mas Eve! His prais - es then I sing;

Then like the sun the star shone forth, And an - gels sang on earth.
For he came down from heav'n a - bove To help a world in need.
And still he loves his lit - tle ones And hears them when they pray.
He o - pens now for ev - 'ry child The pal - ace of the king.

Text: Marie Wexelsen, 1832–1911; tr. Peter A. Sveeggen, 1881–1959; Tune: Peder Knudsen, 1819–1863. Text copyright Augsburg Publishing House.

AWAY IN A MANGER

1 A - way in a man - ger, no crib for his bed, The lit - tle Lord
2 The cat - tle are low - ing; the poor ba - by wakes, But lit - tle Lord
3 Be near me, Lord Je - sus; I ask you to stay Close by me for -

Je - sus laid down his sweet head; The stars in the sky . . looked
Je - sus no cry - ing he makes. I love you, Lord Je - sus; look
ev - er and love me, I pray. Bless all the dear chil - dren in

down where he lay, The lit - tle Lord Je - sus a - sleep on the hay.
down from the sky And stay by my cra - dle till morn - ing is nigh.
your ten - der care And fit us for heav - en to live with you there.

Text: American, 1885. Tune: American, 19th century. Setting: Copyright 1978 *Lutheran Book of Worship*.

GO TELL IT ON THE MOUNTAIN

Go tell it on the moun - tain, O - ver the hills and ev - 'ry - where;

Go tell it on the moun - tain That Je - sus Christ is born!

1 While shep - herds kept their watch - ing O'er si - lent flocks by night, Be -
2 The shep - herds feared and trem - bled When, lo, a - bove the earth Rang
3 Down in a lone - ly man - ger The hum - ble Christ was born; And

hold, through - out the heav - ens There shone a ho - ly light.
out the an - gel cho - rus That hailed our Sav - ior's birth.
God sent us sal - va - tion That bless - ed Christ - mas morn.

Text: Negro spiritual, refrain; John W. Work Jr., 1871–1925, stanzas, alt. Tune: Negro spiritual.

Debbie Trafton O'Neal lives with her husband, three daughters, and assorted pets in Federal Way, Washington. She writes: "Preserving and building family traditions is what makes family get-togethers so much fun. But adding a new twist to traditions that have been passed down through generations is what helps give them a timeless quality." Every Christmas, Debbie and her family have fun with favorite traditions, old and new.

Margy H. Ronning, formerly an artist and designer for Hallmark Cards, lives in Prairie Village, Kansas with her husband Eric, sons Mark and David, and Little Bear their dog. By using a variety of patterns in her artwork she hopes to create a sense of the magic of the Christmas season.

PROTECTED BY ANGELS, A YOUNG TREE GROWS STRONG AND
BEAUTIFUL, THE PRIDE OF THE FOREST—UNTIL IT IS HEWN DOWN
TO SERVE A HIGHER, NOBLER PURPOSE.

The First Christmas Tree

EUGENE FIELD

*American journalist and poet Eugene Field was born in St. Louis, Missouri in 1850. Among his
numerous articles and books are the beloved children's poems "Little Boy Blue" and "Wynken, Blynken,
and Nod," which remain favorites to this day. Field died in Chicago on November 4, 1895.*

*Much of Eugene Field's childhood was spent with relatives in New England. His recollections of
visits to his grandmother in Vermont capture her fierce New England faith, which made a deep
impression on young Field and influenced his later writing: "My lovely old grandmother was one of
the very elect. . . . Yes, Grandma was puritanical, but a Puritan in the severity of her faith and in the
exacting nicety of her interpretation of her duties to God and mankind. Grandma's Sunday began at
six o'clock Saturday evening; by that hour her house was swept and garnished, and her lamps
trimmed, every preparation made for a quiet, reverential observance of the Sabbath Day."*

ONCE UPON A TIME THE FOREST WAS IN A great commotion. Early in the evening the wise old cedars had shaken their heads ominously and predicted strange things. They had lived in the forest many, many years; but never had they seen such marvelous sights as were to be seen now in the sky, and upon the hills, and in the distant village.

"Pray tell us what you see," pleaded a little vine; "we who are not as tall as you can behold none of these wonderful things. Describe them to us, that we may enjoy them with you."

"I am filled with such amazement," said one of the cedars, "that I can hardly speak. The whole sky seems to be aflame, and the stars appear to be dancing among the clouds; angels walk down from heaven to the earth, and enter the village or talk with the shepherds upon the hills."

The vine listened in mute astonishment. Such things never before had happened. The vine trembled with excitement. Its nearest neighbor was a tiny tree, so small it scarcely ever was noticed; yet it was a very beautiful little tree, and the vines and ferns and mosses and other humble residents of the forest loved it dearly.

"How I should like to see the angels!" sighed the little tree, "and how I should like to see the stars dancing among the clouds! It must be very beautiful!"

As the vine and the little tree talked of these things, the cedars watched with increasing interest the wonderful scenes over and beyond the confines of the forest. Presently they thought they heard music, and they were not mistaken, for soon the whole air was full of the sweetest harmonies ever heard upon earth.

"What beautiful music!" cried the little tree. "I wonder whence it comes."

"The angels are singing," said a cedar, "for none but angels could make such sweet music."

"But the stars are singing, too," said another cedar; "yes, and the shepherds on the hill join in the song, and what a strangely glorious song it is!"

The trees listened to the singing, but they did not understand its meaning: it seemed to be an anthem, and it was of a Child that had been born; but further than this they did not understand. The strange and glorious song continued all the night; and all the angels walked to and fro, and the shepherd-folk talked with the angels, and the stars danced and caroled in the high heaven. And it was nearly morning when the cedars cried out, "They are coming to the forest!" And, surely enough, this was true. The vine and the little tree were terrified, and they begged their older and stronger neighbors to protect them from harm. But the cedars were too busy with their own fears to pay any heed to the faint pleadings of the humble vine and the little tree.

The angels came into the forest, singing the same glorious anthem about the Child, and the stars sang in chorus with them, until every part of the woods rang with the echoes of that wondrous song. There was nothing in the appearance of this angel host to inspire fear; they were clad all in white, and there were crowns upon their fair heads, and golden harps in their hands; love, hope, charity, compassion, and joy beamed from their beautiful faces, and their presence seemed to fill the forest with a divine peace. The angels came through the forest to where the little tree

stood, and gathering around it, they touched it with their hands, and kissed its little branches, and sang even more sweetly than before. And their song was about the Child, the Child, the Child that had been born. Then the stars came down from the skies and danced and hung upon the branches of the tree, and they, too, sang that song—the song of the Child. And all the other trees and the vines and the ferns and the mosses beheld in wonder; nor could they understand why all these things were being done, and why this exceeding honor should be shown the little tree.

> *The stars came down and hung upon the branches of the tree, and they, too, sang that song—the song of the Child.*

When the morning came the angels left the forest—all but one angel, who remained behind and lingered near the little tree. Then a cedar asked: "Why do you tarry with us, holy angel?" And the angel answered: "I stay to guard this little tree, for it is sacred, and no harm shall come to it."

The little tree felt quite relieved by this assurance, and it held up its head more confidently than ever before. And how it thrived and grew, and waxed in strength and beauty! The cedars said they never had seen the like. The sun seemed to lavish its choicest rays upon the little tree, heaven dropped its sweetest dew upon it, and the winds never came to the forest that they did not forget their rude manners and linger to kiss the little tree and sing it their prettiest songs. No danger ever menaced it, no harm threatened; for the angel never slept—through the day and through the night the angel watched the little tree and protected it from all evil. Oftentimes the trees talked with the angel; but of course they understood little of what he said, for he spoke always of the Child who was to become the Master; and always when thus he talked, he caressed the little tree, and stroked its branches and leaves, and moistened them with his tears. It all was so very strange that none in the forest could understand.

So the years passed, the angel watching his blooming charge. Sometimes the beasts strayed toward the little tree and threatened to devour its tender foliage; sometimes the woodman came with his ax, intent upon hewing down the straight and comely thing; sometimes the hot, consuming breath of drought swept from the south, and sought to blight the forest and all its verdure: the angel kept them from the little tree. Serene and beautiful it grew, until now it was no longer a little tree, but the pride and glory of the forest.

One day the tree heard someone coming through the forest. Hitherto the angel had hastened to its side when men approached; but now the angel strode away and stood under the cedars yonder.

"Dear angel," cried the tree, "can you not hear the footsteps of someone approaching? Why do you leave me?"

"Have no fear," said the angel; "for He who comes is the Master."

The Master came to the tree and beheld it. He placed His hands upon its smooth trunk and branches, and the tree was thrilled with a strange and glorious delight. Then He stooped and kissed the tree, and then He turned and went away.

Many times after that the Master came to the forest, and when He came, it always was to where the tree stood. Many times He rested beneath the tree and enjoyed the shade of its foliage, and listened to the music of the wind as it swept through the rustling leaves. Many times he slept there, and the tree watched over Him, and the forest was still, and all its voices were hushed. And the angel hovered near like a faithful sentinel.

Ever and anon men came with the Master to the forest, and sat with Him in the shade of the tree, and talked with Him of matters which the tree never could understand; only it heard that the talk was of love and charity and gentleness, and it saw that the Master was beloved and venerated by the others. It heard them tell of the Master's goodness and humility—how He had healed the sick and raised the dead and bestowed inestimable

blessings wherever He walked. And the tree loved the Master for His beauty and His goodness; and when He came to the forest it was full of joy, but when He came not it was sad. And the other trees of the forest joined in its happiness and its sorrow, for they, too, loved the Master. And the angel always hovered near.

The Master came one night alone into the forest, and His face was pale with anguish and wet with tears, and He fell upon His knees and prayed. The tree heard Him, and all the forest was still, as if it were standing in the presence of death. And when the morning came, lo! the angel had gone.

Then there was a great confusion in the forest. There was a sound of rude voices, and a clashing of swords and staves. Strange men appeared, uttering loud oaths and cruel threats, and the tree was filled with terror. It called aloud for the angel, but the angel came not.

"Alas," cried the vine, "they have come to destroy the tree, the pride and glory of the forest!"

The forest was sorely agitated, but it was in vain. The strange men plied their axes with cruel vigor, and the tree was hewn to the ground. Its beautiful branches were cut away and cast aside, and its soft, thick foliage was strewn to the tenderer mercies of the winds.

"They are killing me!" cried the tree; "why is not the angel here to protect me?"

But no one heard the piteous cry—none but the other trees of the forest; and they wept, and the little vine wept too.

Then the cruel men dragged the despoiled and hewn tree from the forest, and the forest saw that beauteous thing no more.

But the night wind that swept down from the City of the Great King that night to ruffle the bosom of distant Galilee, tarried in the forest awhile to say that it had seen that day a cross upraised on Calvary—the tree on which was stretched the body of the dying Master. ✎

Chaska, Minnesota artist Lee Christiansen has been creating illustrations for a wide range of clients for seventeen years. He rendered the illustrations for "The First Christmas Tree" with pastels on a sanded pastel paper surface.

Journeys

Betsy Humphreys

Abraham

Sand grits inside my thongs
Sucks at each step to prolong our trek
Whips into sweat pores, 'round turbaned folds.
God, You promised and I believe,
But is my wandering life a hoax?
Where is rest for this aging fool?
When does faith let me shake my sandals clean?

Lead me to the land of milk and honey
Where my creatures and I may feast
And I am home at last.

Moses

Not only to go, as God commands,
But to lead, as God commands.

"I am nobody. Send someone else,
Send someone with a voice,
Someone not wanted for murder."

"I shall be with you."

I went.

From glorious escape to inglorious desert meandering,
From people rejoicing that Yahweh had visited
To people regretting that dark masters were fled.

"Stand firm," this nobody said.
"Stand firm to see the Promised Land."

Mary and Joseph

Mary and Joseph are small town folk,
Their lives bound by the space
One can walk in a day.
They are settlers, not desert nomads,
But they must go to the city.

They would rather stay home,
Home, where the evening broth is warm,
Where the sweet, woody smells
Of Joseph's shop fill the senses.
But they must go to the city.

So many people, faces unknown.
Her ache, his worry, obscured by crowds.
Yet in a stable, their lives affirmed
Mary and Joseph, in the city.

Caesar's message and God's message
Side by side,
One fulfilled by might,
One by love.

MAGI

Legend says we are three
But we are legion,
And our search by starlight
A wild chase after a dream.

Across uncharted miles of sand
Shifting, deceiving, foreign,
With baby gifts in hand
Doubting our own sanity, as others do.

Suddenly we are kneeling,
Warmed by an infant's gurgling,
Musty, earthy, stable pungence for incense.
The arid journey is watered at last.

YOU AND I

To take a journey and not check the time,
To know what to pack and what to leave behind,
To trek the desert of the soul
With no highlighted map,
To allow for wrong turns and retracing,
To let the plan unfold
Not demanding knowledge of conclusion,
To believe in unseen realities.

We travel a mysterious but historic road,
From Ur of Chaldees to Canaan,
From Egypt to a Promised Land,
From carpenter's shop to noisome city,
From eastern desert to straw-lined manger.
From our world to His.

We journey to catch a piece of the vision,
Each step, each stumble, each blister matched
By the promise and now reality of God.
Journey ending and journey beginning.

Betsy Humphreys of Granite Falls, North Carolina, writes: "The idea of life being a spiritual journey is not new, but it took on personal meaning for me in a small group study on Abraham. The risk and hardship he endured were balanced by hope and promise. I began to see my own journey as a deliberate, but not predefined, search. Right now my personal trek includes writing, listening, walking, volunteering, and teaching in the North Carolina foothills."

New York City illustrator Tanja Butler writes: "Biblical narratives have been the subject of my painting and printmaking for more than twenty years. I enjoyed creating a light-filled watercolor of an American countryside for these figures to inhabit, a reminder that their journey parallels our own. I added a fox in its hole and a nesting bird as I thought of the traveler who promised to always accompany us."

THE SIMPLE, SELF-TAUGHT STYLES OF THREE FOLK ARTISTS CAPTURE
THE WONDER OF GOD'S LOWLY BIRTH AMONG US.

Scenes from Nativity

by Three American Folk Artists

PHILLIP GUGEL

Dutch Colonial, Mexican American, and African American traditions inspired these three works by formally untrained artists. Wonderful examples of a style in American art with a rich, though relatively unknown history, their appeal lies in the direct and simple ways they depict portions of the Nativity.

The Christmas message is proclaimed not only through works of the master European painters whom we often return to during this season, but also through the humble expressions of folk artists such as these. Their simple and reverent images draw forth our awe and wonder at the mystery of God's lowly birth among us.

∼ EARLY 18TH CENTURY ∼

THIS PAINTER, POSSIBLY FROM SCHENECTADY in New York's Hudson River Valley, combines the Magi's visit with that of seven soldiers and two children. The figures of soldiers and children may seem out of place until we recall St. Matthew's account of how King Herod sent soldiers to kill all infant boys. The inclusion of the seemingly benign soldiers reminds us of darker events that would shadow Jesus' birth and life on earth.

In a departure from his usual portrayal as a passive, elderly figure, a young Joseph takes an active part with Mary in presenting the Christ child to the Magi.

Light from the star streams toward the infant, signifying Jesus' divine purpose as well as the beacon that guided the Magi. Because it shines from a blue and pink morning sky, the star seems an astronomical oddity. The donkey gazes in wonder at the miraculous star, adding an amusing note to the scene.

The censer swung by the elderly magus symbolizes the act of worship as well as referring to his gift of frankincense. Following the tradition that one Magi was African, the artist depicts the youngest regal visitor with dark skin.

The soldiers' poses against a backdrop of their furled flag, halberd, and spears, recall group portraits of Dutch militia companies painted during the seventeenth century.

The doll-like figures whose clothing hangs in clumsy folds, the figures' awkward positioning on the ground, and the contrived architectural features, betray the artist's self-taught approach.

Despite these faults, however, the decorative patterns on the wall near the animals and on the soldiers' shields, the use of deep, warm colors, and the mood of quiet reverence imbue this painting with rich and lasting appeal.

The Adoration of the Magi
Artist Unknown. *The Adoration of the Magi*. Abby Aldrich Rockefeller Folk Art Center, Williamsburg, Virginia.

José rafael aragón worked as an itinerant painter in the towns of what is now northern New Mexico. His painting shows the holy family as refugees fleeing Bethlehem for the safety of Egypt, an event that follows the Magi's visit in St. Matthew's gospel account.

Mary and the child are mounted on the donkey led by Joseph. A wingless angel accompanies them, providing direction and protection.

Mary's large crown and sharply defined halo signify her importance as the mother of Jesus. The dove hovering above them, a symbol of the Holy Spirit, is an unusual addition to this scene. Bright blues and reds —colors traditionally ascribed to Mary's garments— enliven the panel and contribute to its festive appeal.

A stage-like setting encloses the figures, with scalloped drapery above and the floor hidden behind a floral painting below. Such decorative elements seem an integral part of Aragón's compositions. We might imagine that this scene is part of a Nativity drama presented as a puppet show in one of the communities where Aragón lived.

Its unique shape and rather small size indicate that this panel probably graced a home as an altarpiece. The bold rosette top adds an additional ornamental touch to the panel.

Aragón, who lived from about 1795 until 1862, enjoyed a long and productive career producing sacred paintings and sculpture for churches and homes. More than 300 panel paintings, twelve church altar screens, and numerous sculptures are attributed to him. Much of his legacy is documented or signed. His works are noted for their bold lines, bright contrasting colors, and lively figures.

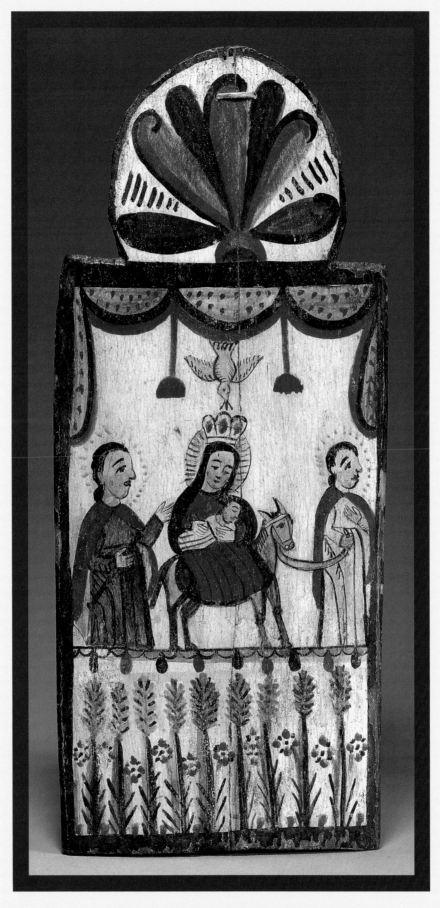

La Huida a Egipto / The Flight into Egypt
José Rafael Aragón. New Mexico, 19th century. Charles D. Carroll Bequest to the Museum of New Mexico,
Museum of International Folk Art, Santa Fe. Photo by Blair Clark.

ELIJAH PIERCE PRACTICED HIS TRIPLE VOCATION as a barber, licensed Baptist lay minister, and wood carver for over fifty years in Columbus, Ohio, after moving there from Baldwyn, Mississippi.

His wife, Cornelia, suggested that he make a book of wood carvings that told the story of Christ's life. This project became his most extensive work. Begun in 1932, it occupied him until his death in 1984.

The book's first page contains six painted panels, carved in low relief, that depict events and persons from the Christmas story. At the top left, a horizontal panel shows the Nativity. Next to it is an illustration of the annunciation to the shepherds. The left middle panel depicts Mary with the infants Jesus and John the Baptist; and the right panel shows the Magi. The unpainted panel on the bottom left presents the first meeting of Jesus and John the Baptist—a rather surprising choice of subject; and the flight to Egypt on the lower right, completes the cycle.

Perhaps John the Baptist had special significance for Pierce, since he appears twice on the book's opening page. John's preaching prepared people for Christ's coming, a task the artist shared through his carvings and words. He once referred to himself as "the man who makes wood talk."

Though Pierce was African American, he did not paint his figures as dark-skinned, choosing instead to depict them as Caucasian. All the figures in his work possess a sense of alertness and immediacy in their attention to the events surrounding them.

Freelance art historian Phillip Gugel lives in St. Paul, Minnesota. In addition to speaking and writing about sacred art, he directs the Capitol Hill Refugee Project, a program that teaches English language skills to adult refugees. This is Gugel's eighteenth consecutive article for *Christmas*.

Book of Wood (First panel, recto)

Elijah Pierce. *Book of Wood* (First panel, recto), c. 1932. Columbus Museum of Art, Ohio; Museum Purchase.

The Christmas I Remember Best

RHEUAMA WEST

*I*T SHOULD HAVE BEEN THE WORST, THE BLEAKEST of Christmases. It turned out to be the loveliest of all my life.

I was nine years old, one of seven children, and we lived in a little farming town in Utah. It had been a tragic year for all of us. But we still had our father, and that made all the difference.

Every year in our town a Christmas Eve Social was held at the church. How well I remember Dad buttoning our coats, placing us all on our long, home-made sleigh and pulling us to the church about a mile away. It was snowing. How cold and good it felt on our faces. We held tight to one another, and above the crunch of snow beneath Dad's feet we could hear him softly whistling "Silent Night."

Mama had died that previous summer. She had been confined to bed for three years, so Dad had assumed all mother and father responsibilities. I remember him standing me on a stool by our big round kitchen table and teaching me to mix bread. But my main task was being Mama's hands and feet until that day in June, her own birthday, when she died. Two months later came the big fire. Our barn, sheds, haystacks, and livestock were destroyed. It was a calamity, but Dad stood between us and the disaster. We weren't even aware of how poor we were. We had no money at all.

I don't remember much about the Christmas Eve Social. I just remember Dad pulling us there and pulling us back. Later, in the front room around our potbellied stove, he served us warm milk and bread. Our Christmas tree, topped by a little worn cardboard angel, had been brought from the nearby hills. Strings of our home-grown popcorn made it the most beautiful tree I had ever seen—or smelled.

After supper Dad had all seven of us sit in a half circle by the tree. I remember I wore a long flannel nightgown. He sat on the floor facing us and told us that he was ready to give us our Christmas gift. We waited, puzzled because we thought Christmas presents were for Christmas morning. Dad looked at our expectant faces. "Long ago," he said, "on a night like this, some poor shepherds were watching their sheep on a lonely hillside. When all of a sudden . . . "

His quiet voice went on and on, telling the story of the Christ child in his own simple words, and I'll never forget how love and gratitude seemed to fill the room. There was light from the oil lamp and warmth from the stove, but somehow it was more than that. We felt Mama's presence. We learned that loving someone was far more important than having something. We were filled with peace and happiness and joy.

When the story was ended Dad had us all kneel for a family prayer. Then he said, "Try to remember, when everything else seems to be lost, the greatest thing of all remains: God's love for us. That's what Christmas means. That's the gift that can never be taken away."

The next morning we found that Dad had whittled little presents for each of us and hung them on the tree, dolls for the girls, whistles for the boys. But he was right: he had given us our real gift the night before.

All this happened long ago, but to this day it all comes back to me whenever I hear "Silent Night" or feel snowflakes on my face, or—best of all—when I get an occasional glimpse of Christ shining in my ninety-year-old father's face. 🖎

This story by Rheuama West, of Spanish Fork, Utah, was the prize-winning essay for a 1972 Christmas feature in Salt Lake City's *Deseret News*. Rheuama West recalls how her story came about: "I was asked to give a surprise tribute to my ninety-year-old father in our church the Sunday before Christmas. As I delivered my speech before the large audience, I could see my dad crying. How well he deserved my sincere tribute. Later, a woman suggested I enter the story in a newspaper contest. I had one day left before the deadline. The next morning, I put it in the mail. Can you imagine my feelings when a phone call told me I had won? This time, *I* cried. Now I could tell the world about my wonderful father."

The work of artist John T. Ward has hung in museums and galleries around the world, including The National Baseball Hall of Fame, The Norman Rockwell Museum, and the U. S. embassy in Swaziland, Africa. Ward calls Saranac Lake, New York in the Adirondack Mountains home.

How Christmas Came to Blueberry Corners

LOIS LENSKI

One of five children of a Lutheran minister, beloved author and artist Lois Lenski was born October 14, 1893 in Springfield, Ohio. Her description of her childhood in Anna, Ohio reflects the color and character she captured in her many books and illustrations: "It was a horse-and-buggy town, automobiles being yet in the future, and life moved at a slow pace. The most familiar sounds were the whistles of a train passing through, the clop-clop of horses' hoofs on the dirt streets, the barking of dogs and the ringing of the church bells. These sounds were, a half-century later, the symbols of a vanished way of life. To have lived it and savored it and been a part of it, has given me great comfort through ensuing years."

In 1946, she received the prized Newbery Medal for her book, Strawberry Girl. *Lois Lenski died in 1974.*

"Do you have gingerbread every day, Julie Ann Janeway?" asked Becky. "With icing on it?"

"Yes," said Julie Ann. "Here, you can have it. I'm sick of gingerbread."

"Don't want it," said Becky, turning her back and walking on. The two girls were walking slowly along the country road that led from the 5th District School to the village a mile away. Behind them followed a group of younger children, including Becky's sister, Fanny, her brother, Abner, and others.

Julie Ann Janeway was a new girl at a new school. She came from Hartford and had never lived in the country before. She wore a satin apron embroidered with flowers; her pantalettes had lace ruffles. On her head, instead of a shawl, she wore a velvet bonnet with a plume on one side. Everyday at recess she talked and other children listened. Even the way she said her words was different, and she had amazing tales to tell.

It was a day in mid-December, in the year 1840. The air was sharp and there had been a light fall of snow in Connecticut. All the way home, Julie Ann talked of something strange, which she called "Christmas."

"What's that?" asked Becky, drawing in her breath sharply.

"It's the day that the Lord Jesus was born!" said Julie Ann, with an important air. "It comes on the 25th of December and we go to church to see the illumination and we have a tree!"

"But Pa didn't say so!" objected Becky.

"Your Pa?" laughed Julie Ann. "Why should he say so?"

"Guess he's the Parson o' the Ecclesiastical Society o' Blueberry Corners, guess he knows 'bout everything!" Becky drew her breath again in sharp defiance. "But he didn't say nothin' 'bout no Christmas."

"Oh, we don't go to the Meeting House!" said Julie Ann, with lofty condescension. "I meant at the Episcopal Church at Blueberry Center; that's where we go. Oh, I just love Christmas, don't you?"

"I never saw one—what are they like?" asked Becky, her curiosity getting the better of her. She might well have added that she had never heard of one, but she did not.

"Oh, Becky Griswold!" cried Julie Ann, clasping her hands in rapture, "they're the most elegantest things you ever saw! Oh, the tree and the candles and the Yule log and the presents. We find the most beautiful spruce tree and we hang it all over with gold and silver apples. For buds and flowers, all over the branches, we hang sugar almonds, sugar plums, burnt almonds, cinnamons, gumballs, and every kind of confectionery! And around the bottom all kinds of beautiful presents."

"What? Tell us," begged the little children.

"I expect I shall have a pretty wax doll, the prettiest doll that ever was, with a variety of neat little dresses. And a silk cloak with quilted trimmings, and my little brother wants a new stick pony to gallop on. It doesn't matter what it is. Anything can come at Christmas!"

"Well, I wish somebody'd give me a wax doll," cried Becky impulsively. Then she bit her lips, for well she knew they wouldn't. Suddenly it seemed dreadful to be the Parson's children. It meant being poorer than anyone else. There were too many mouths to feed in poor Parson Griswold's home. It was such a big family. There would never be any Christmas there. Becky's eyes filled with tears.

"Here, take a bite of my gingerbread, please!" begged Julie Ann. She came close, put her arm in Becky's and with the other hand pressed the gingerbread upon her.

"Don't Christmas ever come to Blueberry Corners where you live?" asked Julie Ann, when they came to the parting of the ways.

"Of course Christmas comes to our house!" Becky burst out indignantly. Why should Julie Ann have everything, satin aprons, lace pantalettes, and Christmas, too? She was filled with sudden rage and jealousy. "Of course we have Christmas!" Then she turned on her heel and ran. A little later Fanny caught up to her and put her arm around her waist.

"Is it true?" she asked, her eyes shining like stars. "Oh, I do so want to have Christmas! If we could only have one Christmas, that would be enough."

"Course we can't," said Becky, sharply. "We're much too poor. I could just shake you for acting so silly."

Fanny was nine and should have been almost as wise as eleven-year-old Becky, but she wasn't. "Oh, I don't care—I do so want a Christmas—so there!" she wailed.

"Well, we can't have one, and you'd better stop thinking about it!" said Becky.

At the supper table that night, Fanny broke out again: "I'll be glad when Christmas comes!" Her serene faith lighted up her small thin face. Becky tried to kick her under the table with her foot, but could not reach far enough. Besides it was too late. Ma and Aunt Philomela had both heard and so had all the rest of the family, all the little brothers and sisters whose heads and elbows showed above the rim of the long table. They all began to stir and clamor and cry, "Oh, what is it?" and "We want it, too!" and "Tell us about it."

Fanny hid her head in shame. "Julie Ann Janeway told us about it at school," she said in a low voice. "It's coming soon, on the 25th of the month."

"But it's not coming here!" protested Becky. "She never said it was!" She wished Fanny were not so stupid, for she saw by her mother's and aunt's faces that this was a serious matter.

"Nonsense!" said Mrs. Griswold emphatically. "What's this child thinking of? We're not Episcopal, that's why we don't believe in keeping those prayerbook days, like Christmas and Easter."

"But can't we have 'presents' like Julie Ann Janeway?" wailed Fanny.

"Presents!" snapped Aunt Philomela. "What be ye thinkin' of? Here's your Pa and Ma scrimpin' and savin' and workin' their heads off jes to git enough clothin' ter kiver ye and food ter fill ye up and wood enough ter warm ye, and ye want presents!"

When Pa returned from making a sick-call, Ma asked him to explain. He went in to his study, looked through a pile of musty books and then his face turned sober as he spoke. The children folded their hands and listened. "Nobody knows when Christ was born, and there is nothing in the Bible to tell us when to keep Christmas," he said. "The disciples and early Christians did not keep Christmas, and no mention is made of its recognition until after the 4th Century; and then there were some who said it was on the 20th of

May, which is every bit as likely as the 25th of December."

Becky and Fanny looked at each other and wondered what all his big words had to do with Julie Ann's tree and presents.

"It was kept for many years in England," he went on, "but it became a celebration of boisterous revelry, in which people forgot the true meaning of Christ's birth. So when our ancestors came to found New England two hundred years ago, they gave up celebrating all saints' days, along with many other Old World customs and practices, which they disapproved of. It is our duty to walk in the good old ways which they laid down for us. So children, do your duty, be obedient, study your catechism, say your prayers and forget this talk of Christmas."

Becky could not sleep for thinking of Christmas. She knew they could not have it, except by some miracle.

The row of eyes around the room closed in respectful silence, and not a murmur was heard during the reading of the Bible and the prayers which followed.

But Becky could not sleep for thinking of Christmas. She had not understood all her father's statements, but she knew that the idea of Christmas, entrancing and enticing as it seemed, when painted by the glowing words of Julie Ann Janeway, was somehow wrong and forbidden. No, they could not have it, except by some miracle. She folded her hands and prayed earnestly.

The days went by slowly, one after the other. Fanny was not sensible at all, and her blue eyes shone more and more like stars. Every day Becky scolded her, but she and the little brothers and sisters became more and more confident.

Every night Becky prayed. On the night of the 24th, over their supper of bread and mush and applesauce, Becky saw the row of eyes of her brothers and sisters shining with bright expectancy, at the thought of what would happen on the morrow. That night she prayed for a miracle.

When she awoke on Christmas morning, all her dreams faded away. She heard the thumping of clothes in the pounding barrel. It was Monday, wash day, not Christmas. Her mother's voice called her at daylight. The room was very cold. She shivered as she pulled her clothes on hastily. When she went down the steep stairs into the kitchen, nothing was different. There were the usual chores to do, cows to be milked, breakfast to get, children's faces to wash, hair to comb, lunches to pack.

"Shall I put on my best gown?" asked little Fanny, when she came down, supreme in her faith. "Don't we go to Meeting on Christmas?"

"Land sakes!" cried Aunt Philomela. "Is the child crazy? Ain't you forgot that Christmas nonsense yet?"

At the usual time the children were packed off to school with their lunches. They waded in the heavy snow up to their knees. The first thing they noticed was that Julie Ann Janeway was conspicuous by her absence.

Becky Griswold thought hard all morning. By noon she had worked out a philosophy of her own. Nice things have to be worked for, she thought. They do not come of themselves. Christmas will never come if you don't bring it yourself. All the little brothers and sisters were trusting. Becky must make a miracle happen.

At noon, Becky left the school house and started off across a field. Behind her, Fanny called frantically and then came running up, her hair flying.

"Where are you going?" she asked breathlessly.

"I'm going to get Christmas for all of us," said Becky. "Now you must go back and say nothing."

"Oh, Becky, I'm so glad," said Fanny. "I just knew Christmas would come!" Then she ran back to her seat in the schoolroom.

Becky soon left the field and went back to the main road, where walking was easier, for the road had been broken out that morning. When she reached home, she peeped in at the back door. She had one last hope that Christmas might have arrived during her absence. But no—Aunt Philomela and Mis' Buxton, a neighbor, and Ma were spinning wool. She smelled a parsnip stew cooking in the big kettle in the fireplace. She hated parsnip stew. It always meant that there was not enough pork to go around, so they would have to fill up on parsnips.

Becky knew now that she would have to find Christmas herself. Before she reached the woodshed, she made up her mind what she would do. She found a hatchet and hid it under her coat. Becky flew down the hill again, but she did not return to school.

She went to the village, and on the way she passed Julie Ann Janeway's house—a great, white square mansion with green blinds, which sat snugly behind a white picket fence. She hurried past, she did not want to look in. Then suddenly there was Julie at her side, pulling and tugging, dragging her in. Inside the great room, she saw a merry crowd around the table, singing and laughing and eating. In a corner of the next room, she saw the tree, covered with lighted candles. So that was a Christmas tree! She gasped as she looked. It was more beautiful than anything she had ever seen in her life!

Julie Ann wore a silk dress with ruffles, and her hair hung over her shoulders in a shower of curls. She jumped and danced about gaily, pointing out her array of gifts.

Becky held her arms crossed tightly over her thin chest to keep the hatchet from slipping. Her coat was too small for her. Her hands were bare and her wrists showed red and raw below her sleeves. Her little head shawl was tied firmly in a knot under her chin. She stood stiffly and stared. Then she shivered and turned away. Julie Ann pressed a large chunk of candied gingerbread upon her, but she did not take it.

"Don't Christmas ever come to Blueberry Corners?" asked Julie.

"Course it comes!" she cried as she went out the door.

She flew down the road as fast as her thin legs would carry her.

At length she came out in a pasture where many seedling pines had sprung up. She examined the small trees carefully. One was too large, one too small, one bent or crooked. Was there one as pretty as Julie Ann's?

At last she found a perfect tree. It was just a little taller than she was herself. Her hands had grown cold and stiff without mittens. She took the hatchet from under her coat, tied the little head shawl tighter under her chin and began to chop. The trunk of the tree was sturdy and the hatchet slipped and fell against her shoe. Becky looked down at her feet and there in the snow which had been white like the wool on a sheep's back, she saw a spot of bright red. It grew larger and larger as she watched. She looked more closely and then saw that a great gash had been cut in her new calf-skin shoes—the shoes she had worked so hard to earn and which were to last till next summer. Suddenly she hid her face in her hands and burst into tears, then she crumpled up on the ground.

Some time later, she roused herself and could not seem to remember what had happened. She was very cold and stiff and could hardly move. The sun was sinking slowly behind the pine-clad hill. The she saw the tree lying on its side and she remembered. The wind had blown it over. She must hurry and bring Christmas to the children or they would all be disappointed. She tried to get up but she couldn't. Her foot hurt badly. Over the brow of the hill she saw smoke rising from a chimney. It was old Hiram Curtis' cottage, a quarter of a mile away. She began to make her way toward it, crawling by inches.

Becky never knew how she got there, but finally she came in sight of Old Hiram's woodpile. Fortunately, he was there, picking up an armful of wood. He dropped it hastily and came limping, for he was crippled, when he heard her feeble voice calling.

"Wal, ef it ain't Becky Griswold, the Parson's darter, sure's I'm alive, crawlin' along on all fours! Whatever ails ye? Oh, I must call Mirandy, she'll know what ter do. Jes ye wait now."

He limped down the hill as quickly as he could and in a few moments Mirandy came with a wooden sled. The two old people helped Becky onto the sled and dragged it to the back door. Then they carried her in to a bed in the corner of the kitchen and Old Mirandy bandaged up her foot and treated her hands and feet and ears for frost-bite.

Suddenly Becky remembered the tree which she had left on the hillside. She told Old Hiram about it and he went painstakingly after it. By the time he returned, it was dark. The mountain road which led to their cottage had not been broken out and as he had only one poor, lame horse, he could not take her home. Becky's foot began to pain her and finally she fell into a fitful sleep.

That afternoon, when the children came home from school and Becky was not with them, Mrs. Griswold questioned Fanny.

"She went to get our Christmas! She went to get our Christmas!" said Fanny over and over again, her eyes full of tears.

"Still talking foolishness!" snorted Aunt Philomela. "When will that child learn to be sensible!"

By nightfall, Becky's mother was alarmed and anxious. The younger children were put to bed, whimpering. When Parson Griswold returned late in the evening, he too was alarmed. He walked to the nearest neighbor's to make inquiries, but no one had seen Becky. Several men went to the village to ask about her, but returned without success. Mrs. Griswold sat up all night, but Becky did not come.

The next morning, Fanny continued to insist, "She went to get our Christmas!" so Parson Griswold stopped in at the Janeway house. There Julie Ann and Mrs. Janeway told him of Becky's visit on the previous day, but the incident threw no light on her present whereabouts. He left to join the other searchers. Word had spread like wildfire through the little community that Becky Griswold was missing. The village was filled with people running here and there, the Meeting House bell rang fast and furiously. A large search party was set out to scour the woods and hillsides.

After Parson Griswold left the Janeway house, Julie Ann began to cry. "Oh mother," she wailed, "it's all my fault. I was so selfish, I bragged about Christmas all the time, and about all the things I was going to get. It's all my fault that she's lost." Mrs. Janeway took her repentant daughter in her arms; she knew she was being well punished for her misdeeds. "Becky said she never had a tree and never had a present except a hand-me-down petticoat in her whole life," went on Julie Ann in distress. "Oh mother, let's make Christmas all ready for Becky to see when she comes back! I'm sure they'll find her, aren't you? She wanted Christmas so much, and so did Fanny!"

At the parsonage, Mrs. Griswold met many visitors at the door, fresh hope arising with each arrival. "Have you seen her? Have you seen Becky?" she cried over and over. Then, frantic, she fell back again into despair. She threw her apron over her head and sobbed.

"Don't, Ma, please!" said little Fanny. "She'll come, Ma, I know she will. She's just gone to get us a Christmas!" Fanny was the only sensible one now, the only one who did not cry. Her faith never wavered for an instant.

When Mrs. Janeway and Julie appeared at the door, bearing in their arms Julie's beautiful tree and a host of presents, Aunt Philomela sniffed, "Christmas nonsense! We don't hold to that! That's what caused all the trouble!" But she could not refuse them entrance. The other neighbor women crowded round to see and hear when Julie Ann and her mother explained. They were all Meeting House people and had never heard about Christmas, but the idea appealed to them. Worn and anxious with worry and waiting, it gave them something to do. One by one they went home to return again with cakes and gingerbread, pots of beans, baskets of apples, potatoes, groceries, jugs of cider, blankets, clothing and even a few toys for the children.

Christmas day had passed and it was the following afternoon when Becky opened her eyes in the little Curtis cottage. Old Aunt Mirandy sat by her bed and held her hand.

"There, there, now, don't ee move! Hiram's gone ter git a bob-sled from Eddie Coddington," the old woman went on. "We'll git ye home 'fore nightfall."

A half-hour later, the bob-sled came, and with it several strong men. They placed an old mattress on the sled, and Becky was moved onto it and covered with blankets and bear-skins.

"Oh, my tree! My tree!" she cried as they were about to start.

"To be sure! To be sure!" cried Old Hiram. "Ye must have it!" He fastened it up in the front and the sight of its green, waving branches gave her comfort.

On the way home she seemed to rouse from sleep and was surprised to hear bells ringing. There were people, men, women, and children, walking along beside the sled and behind it. The crowd without and within the house gave way as the procession drew up—a bob-sled with a little green pine tree at its head, carrying a sad, limp burden.

Becky was carried by willing hands into the little bedroom which opened off the great central kitchen. She did not open her eyes. The doctor was called and he stayed in the room a long time.

At last, Becky opened her eyes again. Beside her, on a chair, stood a little, green pine tree, without trimming of any kind. She reached out her hand and touched the green needles tenderly. Through the open door, in the corner of the room, stood another tree, laden with gold and silver apples, sugar almonds and sugar plums, cinnamons and gumballs. On the table beneath was piled an array of presents. There were enough for every one of all the little brothers and sisters. As Becky saw all their little heads crowding eagerly about the tree, she felt a deep peace in her heart.

Becky could not understand what happened. It must be a miracle! The miracle she had prayed for so hard.

Her father came and sat by her bedside and the children hushed their voices as he read the story of the birth of Christ and then prayed from a heart overflowing with gratitude. Becky was surprised to see the faces of neighbors peering in from the other room, to see Aunt Philomela wiping tears away from her eyes.

She could not understand what had happened. It was all very strange and too good to be true. It must be a miracle! The miracle she had prayed for so hard.

"Did Christmas come after all?" she asked.

"Yes, child," said her father, "because you brought it. You have shown us the true spirit of Christmas, and from this time on, we will have Christmas every year, for we truly need it."

"So Christmas came to Blueberry Corners after all!" said Becky.

"I knew it would!" said little Fanny, and her eyes shone like stars. ✎

The CHRISTMASTIME OF 50 YEARS AGO.

First appearing in the 1952 edition of the Annual, "The Christmastime of 50 Years Ago" was one of more than twenty such picture stories included in issues of Christmas over the years. Created by illustrator Lee Mero and Randolph Haugen, the Annual's originator, these popular features were, in Haugen's words, "for those to whom the modern holiday season seems to get more glamorous and clamorous each year, but who still experience that old nostalgic feeling for the Christmas of a more quiet, bygone era."

a Picture Story
by
LEE
MERO

FOREWORD

Well, Christmas 50 years ago was celebrated pretty much the same as it is now. Candles were lit; services honored the Birth of the Christ Child; families met around festive firesides; gifts were sent and gifts were received.

But what folks wished for, what they got and what they wore form the background for these pages. There will probably be some "NOT REALLYS" from the youngsters but we hope for some nostalgic "OH! I REMEMBER THATS" from the older generation.

Ye Editor AND Ye Artist

47

CROWDS of SHOPPERS THRONGED THE STREETS JUST AS

Oriental Cozy Corners were prettied up for Open House.

The Eternal Question

"Yes or No?"

Young men, home from College, pinned up their favorite "Gibson Girls"—

Lit the gas light in the Front Hall — (those new mantles were awfully bright)

The Tray for Calling Cards was placed conveniently near the front door.

Rang up their Best Girls —

And Took them on Sleighride Parties!

SKAARSHEIM · LIVERY · STABLE

KENYON Directory

THEY DO TODAY, ❦ Ah, but the STYLES

were somewhat different!

(for instance) Milliner's thought that Plumes "did something" to a Hat! — And men thought Derbies were tops! (no Pun intended)

Hot Chestnuts

The Equivalent of "No Parkin" HERE, MAC

With Company sure to arrive, a new washstand was bought for the spare bedroom!

Extra coats and hats were removed from the hall tree,

The "Mikado Fern Ball" in the dining room window was watered

Sargent's "Frieze of the Prophets" was taken down and the Christmas wreath was hung over the fireplace.

CHRISTMAS ORATORIOS WERE SUNG

Joy to the world, the Lord is come

The most UN-sung role was that of the young man who pumped the organ!

Sunday School Trees were bright with real candles

And in grade schools, Pieces were spoken by little girls and little boys dressed in their "Sunday Best"

But alert watchers stood handy with buckets of water (just in case)

Children received Christmas Stockings

this is a "natty Russian Knickerbocker Suit"

At the closing exercises before the Holidays, the circumspect young ladies of the Junior Class at the Normal School staged their thrilling Wand and Dumb-bell Drill

(from a photo — honest!)

Candles glowed in many a front window.

THERE WAS A PLENTIFUL SUPPLY OF HACKS FOR THOSE ATTENDING CHRISTMAS SERVICES

FOLKS STOPPED TO SING CAROLS AT HOMES OF FRIENDS — And then gathered 'round the Samovar for tea and Cookies.

CHRISTMAS DAY MEANT CHRISTMAS DINNER, with perhaps the Pastor and his family as special guests. And Turkey was the favorite bird, then as now!

I resent that

Popular after-dinner subject with the men was the Boer War.

Children weren't glued to television sets but went bob-sledding and skating

Young Ladies accompanied their favorite tenor on the Pianola.

DOM PAUL

Women talked about the perils of the Missionaries in China, due to the Boxer Rebellion; and the beautiful new Maxfield Parrish prints, the new savory, Onion Salt, men's high collars; Gibson Girls, etc, etc.

EVERYBODY thought those moving pictures were here to stay; perhaps they would TALK some day (laughter); those new automobiles would never take the place of horses **and** maybe something should be done about those "Trusts" being formed and what about that "Free Silver" idea, etc, etc.—

Remember?

The House of Bread

Christmas Eve at Grandma's House

STEVEN SCHOU

Water, grain, salt, and yeast—
the fundamental stuff of bread
and parables.

She doesn't need a cup,
but kneads the leaven in,
and flour and salt,

her fingers know the recipe:
more flour. She sows it in
and kneads again,

then covers it, and in the dark
the leaven grows, like seed,
we know not how.

She sows a bed of flour,
her fingers hold the memory,
and forms a loaf,

then swaddles it in white
and gently lays it in the pan:
the bread of life.

Her fragrant offering
fills the house where young and old
will come tonight,

and she will read how Mary
bore the perfect seed and cradled him
amid the straw
in Bethlehem.

Steven Schou, a pastor in Granville, North Dakota,
explains: "This poem is about my mother and my
grandmother. For as long as I can remember, Mom
has baked bread three times a week, six loaves
each time. This came to mind as I thought about
the Christmas story, because Bethlehem, the site
of Jesus' birth, means 'House of Bread.' The
Christmas traditions I remember begin at Grandma's
house. When I was a child, no one opened presents
until we each had chosen a carol to sing and
Grandma had read the Christmas story."

FOR ONE WONDERFUL DAY, THE SLAVE QUARTERS ON A SOUTHERN
PLANTATION RING WITH SOUNDS OF JOY, HIGH SPIRITS, AND GOOD WILL.

All Day It's Christmas

Christmas in the Quarters

PATRICIA C. MCKISSACK AND FREDRICK L. MCKISSACK

IT'S CHRISTMAS IN THE QUARTERS ALL DAY. After the Christmas gif' exchange at the Big House, the slaves hold a religious service—just long enough to be respectful, but short enough to hold everybody's attention. There's prayer, testimony, singing, and a closing prayer led by an elder: "Lawd, if dancing is wrong in your sight, then I'm asking that you let the time excuse the sin . . . " Then the women hurry back to their cabins, change into work clothes, and start cooking.

The fireplace is used to cook, heat water, and keep the one-room cabin warm. The slave cook hangs a pot on a crane, and sets it at different heights over the coals to regulate the cooking heat. Most of them don't have but one pot and maybe a skillet. And that pot and skillet "is seasoned and knows how to cook" special dishes like gravied rabbit, smoked ham and red-eye gravy, or mixed greens.

In one cabin the pungent smell of red pepper mixed with vinegar delights those who love the spicy flavor of meats prepared this way. Next door, sweet 'taters are roasting in ashes along with a plump, juicy chicken. This is sho' better than leather breeches and fatback.

A mother shows her young helper how to make ashcakes. She teases the shy girl, saying, "Honey, I don't hand my recipes out to just anybody."

First she pours boiling water over cornmeal. The daughter adds a pinch of salt and a bit of molasses. (That's the key ingredient.) They wrap small amounts in cabbage leaves and place them in the ashes. "Best eatin' ever!"

But it's the preparing of the possum that is taken quite seriously. Children sing outside the window where their mother is working:

> *De way to cook de 'possum nice,*
> *Carve him to the heart.*
> *First parbile him, stir him twice,*
> *Carve him to the heart.*
> *Den lay sweet tates in de pan,*
> *Carve him to the heart.*
> *Nuthin' beats dat in the lan',*
> *Carve him to the heart.*

At dusk the meal is laid out on a common table for all to share. Every cook brings her own special dish. Christmas in the Quarters is the one time of the year there's enough to eat, and enough time to enjoy a meal with family and friends.

An elder blesses the food and the "hands that prepared it all." He gives thanks for another year's good health, and remembers those who are sick or passed on. Amen! And the feast begins!

> *Virginny Ham, Roast Chicken, Chitlings, Squirrel*
> *Pickled Pig Feet*
> *Possum and Sweet Potatoes*
> *Poke Salad Greens and Eggs*
> *Cabbage, Squash, and Wild Greens*
> *   Cooked with Ham Hocks*
> *Ashcakes*
> *Buttermilk, Sassafras Tea,*
> *   and Persimmon Wine (homemade)*

After the big meal in the Quarters, gifts are presented. Santa visited the children earlier, but slave mothers usually give their children something personal, like an apron, basket, a strip quilt, or a hat. They attach a story or advice to it, so if they are separated by being sold, one from the other, the children will have a memory:

"My mama, your grandmama, made me this apron and told me if I ever had a daughter to pass it on to her. I'm giving it to you now that you're twelve. Keep it clean, like your thoughts and deeds."

Then one of the elders is singled out and given a gift of appreciation from all the neighbors in the Quarters. A hat, a pipe, some tobacco, a carved walking stick draw oohs and aahs and a few tears.

The music starts and the dancing begins. The folk that don't hold with dancing on Christmas Day, and especially on Sunday, go some distance away to hold religious services or "pit school." Still other slaves choose not to join in. They have freedom on their minds: "We eat at Christmas and our bellies scream for food all the rest of the year. Let us not forget Dangerfield Newby and the men who died at Harpers Ferry trying to free us. We should free ourselves!" ✒

Sweet Potato Pie (Slave Style)

Two big sweet potatoes grown in the garden patch out back

2 cups of sugar (trade with the Big House cook). If not available use 1 cup of molasses or honey

¼ pound of butter. Scrape from the insides of the butter churn

2 tsp. vanilla

1 tsp. of cinnamon

½ tsp. nutmeg

If you can't get spices then use a tablespoon of rum

½ cup of milk, if somebody you know gets to milk the cow

4 eggs. Send the children to gather eggs in the hay

Peel cooked sweet potatoes and mash them together with butter, sugar, and spices. Beat eggs and milk together in a separate bowl, then slowly add mixture to the potatoes. Beat mixture briskly until it is creamy and smooth.

Pour potatoes into a pie crust shell. Cook until firm. If you can stick a knife in the middle of the pie and none of the mixture sticks, it is ready. Serve after it has cooled.

Wife and husband, Patricia C. and Fredrick L. McKissack, have written nearly 100 books and won numerous awards for their writing. While both have created books on their own, they collaborate on many projects. "One of the reasons we write for children is to introduce them to African and African-American history and historical figures. . . . We want them to feel the tremendous amount of hurt and sadness that racism and discrimination cause all people, regardless of race," Fred explains. A favorite project was researching *Christmas in the Big House, Christmas in the Quarters*, which took them through the states of Virginia, West Virginia, and Tennessee. The McKissacks live in St. Louis, Missouri.

Though he lost an eye as a child, illustrator Tim Ladwig always loved to draw. He studied drawing in Italy and has worked for seventeen years as an inner city community minister. Ladwig has illustrated eight books including *Probity Jones and the Fear Not Angel*. He lives with his family in Wichita, Kansas.

Simple Gifts

Pamela Johnson and Sandra Burrowes

Gifts made with our hands are gifts filled with love and imagination. They recall a time when life was simpler. And, in the love and care we put into them, they reflect the real spirit of Christmas giving: the love God declares by becoming a baby in our midst. This Christmas season, let the story of Jesus' birth be the center of your thoughts as you snip and trim, sew and bake easy-to-make, wonderfully nostalgic handmade gifts.

59

Remember the Magi's costly gifts of gold, frankincense, and myrrh as you make these elegant gift decanters of fragrant, colorful vinegars— all wrapped in luxurious satin and velvet bags.

Golden Herbed Vinegar

The striking color of this aromatic vinegar makes it a pleasure to the eye as well as the palate. A few sprigs of your favorite fresh herbs—thyme, rosemary, or mint—combined with garlic and lemon peel, add a wonderful gourmet touch. Fill lovely new or old bottles, cork them, and festoon them with ribbon before slipping each into its own gift bag.

INGREDIENTS

sprigs of fresh thyme

sprigs of fresh rosemary

large cloves of garlic

strips of lemon peel

cider or white wine vinegar

thin wooden skewers

INSTRUCTIONS

Place a sprig of thyme and rosemary into each bottle. Thread a strip of lemon peel along the length of a thin wooden skewer. Next, spear the skewer through a garlic clove and place it into the bottle with the herbs. Fill bottle with vinegar and cover. Allow to steep at least one week to bring out the flavors.

Cranberry Vinegar

The refreshing tartness of cranberries blends with honey and cinnamon to flavor this unique and festive vinegar.

INGREDIENTS

1 quart of cider or white wine vinegar

2 cups fresh or frozen cranberries

1/2 cup clover honey or flavored honey such as orange blossom

whole cloves

cinnamon sticks

INSTRUCTIONS

Combine vinegar and one cup of berries in a saucepan. Bring to a boil, reduce heat, and simmer for two minutes. Remove from heat, add honey, and stir well. Strain into a large measuring cup or pitcher.

Divide remaining berries between two clean 16-ounce decorative bottles or four 8-ounce bottles. Place whole cloves and one cinnamon stick in each bottle. Fill bottles with warm vinegar and cover. Prepare at least a week in advance so flavor mellows.

Now when Jesus was born in Bethlehem of Judaea in the day, Jerusalem . . . and when they had opened their treasures, the

Bag for Vinegar Decanter

MATERIALS

½ yard of both fabric and lining

thread

corded tassel or ribbon

INSTRUCTIONS

Cut a 5-½" circle from both fabric and lining. This will form the base. Cut a rectangle 19" wide by 14" tall from both fabric and lining. Fold the fabric rectangle in half with right sides together to form a cylinder. Sew a ½" side seam along the 14" side. Repeat for lining. Sew the fabric base to the fabric cylinder, right sides together, using ½" seam. Repeat for the lining fabric. Turn fabric cylinder right side out. Fold over and press ½" of the open edge of the fabric cylinder to the inside. Leaving lining cylinder wrong-side out, fold over and press ½" of the open edge to the outside. Place the lining cylinder into the fabric cylinder, wrong sides together. Line up the pressed edges and stitch together, using a decorative stitch (this will show when the lining is cuffed over). Place the bottle in the bag, cuff the edge over to reveal lining. Secure with a corded tassel or ribbon.

Trinket Bag

MATERIALS

½ yard of both fabric and lining

thread

corded tassel (available in upholstery section of fabric stores)

INSTRUCTIONS

With right sides together, cut a large circle, three times the diameter of the object being wrapped, from both fabric and lining. Pin edges with right sides still together. Sew around circumference of the circle, using ½" seam and leaving a 2" opening for turning. Clip curved edge. Turn the material right side out and press. Blind-hem the seam closed. Wrap the gift by placing it in the center of circle, gathering the edges, and tying with corded tassel.

*f Herod the king, behold, there came wise men from the east to
resented unto him gifts: gold, and frankincense, and myrrh.*

MATTHEW 2:1, 11b

In Victorian America, pomanders were treasured gifts. Usually made from oranges and whole cloves, they remind us of the Bethlehem shepherds, whose humble lives were tied to the fruits of the land.

This variation on those pomanders makes an elegant, scented ornament. With a polystyrene ball as its base, it will add a touch of Christmas to the air long after the holiday is over.

Pomander Ornaments

MATERIALS

Walnuts, almonds, miniature pinecones, dried rosehips, whole nutmegs, whole allspice, filberts, pecans, cloves (choose as many as you like for decorations)

polystyrene balls (available at craft stores)

metallic paint in gold, bronze, or copper (optional)

hot glue gun (available at craft or hardware stores)

INSTRUCTIONS

Select polystyrene ball in the desired size. Using a glue gun, carefully attach nuts to the ball in a decorative design of your choice. (For a more dramatic look, you may gild the nuts before applying them to the ball. Allow paint to dry thoroughly before gluing.)

Glue smaller decorations—allspice, tiny pinecones, nutmegs, rosehips—into empty spaces on the ornament so that none of the ball is visible.

For a stunning presentation, arrange several pomanders of different sizes and trims among greenery on a mantel or in a bowl. Or wrap the pomanders with bands of ribbon for a truly elegant gift.

And there were in the same country shepherds abiding in the field, keeping watch over their flock by night.

LUKE 2:8

Here is a simple and unusual cake that could have come out of many kitchens in colonial America. It has just the right amount of sweetness and a rich, hearty texture—a cake fit for Christmas angels! Wrap individual pieces in plastic wrap tied with colorful bows, or give an entire cake, cut and arranged on a festive holiday plate.

Angel Honey Cake with Almonds

4 eggs
1 cup sugar
¼ cup vegetable oil
1 cup honey
1 tablespoon instant coffee
½ cup boiling water
3 cups flour
1½ teaspoons baking powder
½ teaspoon baking soda
¼ teaspoon ground cinnamon
1 cup chopped almonds
  grated peel of one orange

In a large bowl, beat the eggs until frothy. Gradually add the sugar and beat for 30 seconds. Add the vegetable oil and honey. Beat for 30 seconds. Dissolve the instant coffee in the boiling water and add to the mixing bowl. Add the flour, baking powder, soda, and cinnamon, beating until well combined. Fold in the almonds and orange peel. Pour into a greased and waxed-paper-lined 9 x 13 x 2" pan. Bake in a 325° oven for 50 minutes. When done, invert the cake on a wire rack. Cool. Remove the waxed paper and wrap in aluminum foil to keep fresh.

And suddenly there was with the angel a multitude of the heavenly host praising God, and saying, "Glory to God in the highest, and on earth peace, good will."

LUKE 2: 13, 14

Pamela Johnson is Director of Product Management on the Augsburg Fortress book team. She loves to give big "theme parties"—just ask her daughter and new son-in-law! This past May, in an outdoor cere-mony hosted by Pamela and her husband, they were married in a fully-blooming apple orchard, complete with huge baskets of garden flowers, tangy summer salads, and yards and yards of streaming purple and blue ribbons.

Sandra Burrowes is the mother of two young children and marketing manager for the Augsburg Fortress book team. Time is short for working mothers, but she makes time every other week for "Craft Night"—an opportunity to gather with friends to socialize and to work on her latest project, be it invitations for one of the kid's birthday parties or the elegant pomanders found on these pages.

Photographer Leo Kim spent time in Shanghai, Macao, Hong Kong, and Austria before coming to the United States to study architecture and design. He currently lives and works in Minneapolis, Minnesota.

Christmas Memories

How We Spent Christmas Eve

_____

Christmas Day Highlights

_____

Family Christmas Traditions in Our Home

_____

Favorite Gifts

_____

Our Holiday Guests   *Their Greetings and Wishes*

_____   _____

_____   _____

_____   _____

(Attach a Christmas photo here.)

The creator of the border art on this page and on page three of this year's annual, Kenn Backhaus, was born and raised on his family's farm in Wisconsin and has always been inspired by the outdoors. His favorite methods of capturing color, value, and mood are painting on location or through direct observation. He explains: "I want the viewer to feel and see the end of each brush stroke, to understand what I might have felt in painting it. The paint brush allows me freedom to record the ever changing moods that make up life's harmonies."